BREAKING FREE FROM CHURCHIANITY

HOW TO LIVE FREE FROM RELIGIOUS LEGALISM, DESTRUCTIVE DOGMA, AND PEOPLE-PLEASING IN CHURCHES

SCOTT COOK

TWS | THE WRITER'S SOCIETY PUBLISHING

© Copyright 2024 by D. Scott Cook - All rights reserved.

All rights reserved. No part of this publication may be reproduced, stored in a retrieval system, or transmitted in any form or by any means — electronic, mechanical, digital, photocopy, recording, or any other — except for brief quotations in printed reviews without the publisher's prior permission.

NO AI TRAINING: Without in any way limiting the author's [and publisher's] exclusive rights under copyright, any use of this publication to "train" generative artificial intelligence (AI) technologies to generate text is expressly prohibited. The author reserves all rights to license uses of this work for generative AI training and development of machine learning language models.

The author of this book does not dispense medical advice or prescribe the use of any technique as a form of treatment for physical, emotional, or medical problems without the advice of a physician, either directly or indirectly. The intent of the author is only to offer information of a general nature to help you in your quest for emotional and spiritual well-being. In the event you use any of the information in this book for yourself, the author and the publisher assume no responsibility for your actions.

Scripture quotations marked ESV are taken from the ESV® Bible (The Holy Bible, English Standard Version®), copyright © 2001 by Crossway, a publishing ministry of Good News Publishers. Used by permission. All rights reserved. The ESV text may not be quoted in any publication made available to the public by a Creative Commons license. The ESV may not be translated into any other language.

Scripture taken from the New King James Version®. Copyright © 1982 by Thomas Nelson. Used by permission. All rights reserved.

Scripture quoted by permission. Quotations designated NET are from the NET Bible® copyright ©1996, 2019 by Biblical Studies Press, L.L.C. http://netbible.com. All rights reserved.

All Scripture marked with the designation "GW" is taken from GOD'S WORD®. © 1995, 2003, 2013, 2014, 2019, 2020 by God's Word to the Nations Mission Society. Used by permission.

Scripture taken from the New King James Version® marked NKJV. Copyright © 1982 by Thomas Nelson. Used by permission. All rights reserved.

Scripture quotations marked (KJV) are taken from the Holy Bible, King James Version (Public Domain in America).

Scripture quotations marked (CEV) are from the Contemporary English Version Copyright © 1991, 1992, 1995 by American Bible Society. Used by permission.

The author adds all italicized emphasis in Scripture quotations.

This book includes stories in which people's names and some details of their situations have been changed.

All internal diagram art is produced by the author of the book.

Library of Congress Cataloging-in-Publication Data is available upon request.

PAPERBACK: ISBN 978-1-961180-37-6

TWS | The Writer's Society Publishing
Lodi, CA
www.thewriterssociety.online

To my brother who was the first to warn me about the dangers of religion.

CONTENTS

Preface	ix
Introduction	xiii
Part One	xvii
1. The Paradox of Christian Religion: "Churchianity"	1
2. Religious Codependency	11
3. The Suffering of Enlightenment	23
4. The Call to Spiritual Freedom	33
Part Two	41
5. Beyond Denominations and Dogma	43
6. Love Heretic	55
7. Reconsidering Core Theological Beliefs: Part One	67
8. Reconsidering Core Theological Beliefs: Part Two	79
9. Leaving the Tribe of My Father and Mother	89
Part Three	99
10. Freedom to Love Yourself	101
11. Freedom to Love Everyone	111
12. From Churchianity to Spiritual Freedom	121
13. Open-Mindedness Unlocks the Door to Spiritual Freedom	137
Afterword	145
Notes	155
Acknowledgments	159
About the Author	161
Also by Scott Cook	163

PREFACE

Over the last thirty years, I have become aware of religion's deficiencies, control, and manipulations. It took years, but I accepted the truth of the shortcomings and failures of my denomination and the Christian religion in general. Breaking away from a denominational religious bubble is tough; it took a traumatic event, a big "aha" moment for me.

I stopped attending church during the COVID-19 lockdowns and never returned. Having Sundays to myself allowed me to accomplish more during the weekend and I felt refreshed and ready for the week. More than that, a culmination of change in my theology and outlook on life caused me not to go back.

As a senior pastor, I was critical of people who left the religious organized institution of "church" as though they had betrayed Christ and the gospel. I had witnessed some who left because they didn't get their way or the pastor somehow hurt their feelings. Others, I discovered, were never genuinely interested in being there. Some left only after careful deliberation, prayer, contemplation, and scriptural study; this described me.

Many people, like me, are breaking away from religious denominationalism, as I call it. Breaking away to reframe and deconstruct beliefs. Only then can their beliefs be built on the reality of God's unconditional love, complete grace, and unending compassion.

Whatever your reason for reading this, I hope it will give you a greater understanding of the limits of the religious bubble and help you begin the process of deconstruction and healing on the road to spiritual freedom.

My title, *Breaking Free from Churchianity*, may seem binary to some, as if a person couldn't be involved in a Christian church and experience spiritual freedom and health simultaneously. I understand the argument and know people who continue to participate in a denominational church due to their convictions and beliefs while deconstructing their theology and seeking emotional healing and spiritual freedom. However, Jesus put it this way:

> *"... 'No one tears a piece from a new garment and puts it on an old garment. If he does, he will tear the new, and the piece from the new will not match the old. And no one puts new wine into old wineskins. If he does, the new wine will burst the skins and it will be spilled, and the skins will be destroyed. But new wine must be put into fresh wineskins. And no one after drinking old wine desires new, for he says, 'The old is good.'" Luke 5:36-39 ESV*

The old wine symbolized the Law of Moses, as detailed in the Torah. In contrast, the new wine represented the new covenant, rooted in the grace found in Jesus' life and finished work, rather than relying on circumcision and strict adherence to the Mosaic law. However, the religious leaders clung to the familiar taste of the old covenant, desiring to continue living by its principles — much like attempting to pour old wine into new wineskins. Jesus, on the other hand, presented them with the new wine of radical grace through His finished work, distinctly separate from their efforts; this was the essence of the new covenant in Him.

If you opt to remain within the Western evangelical system, anticipate encountering the associated drawbacks and prevailing old mindsets in today's Christian religious framework. This situation mirrors the challenges faced by early believers after the resurrection, as they grappled with the pressures of participating in the synagogue and temple rituals linked to the old covenant. (Refer to the book of Hebrews for a more detailed explanation of this difficulty.)

Can you stay in the old Christian religious system? Yes. Should you? That is a personal decision only you can make. As for me, I have found greater freedom and growth outside the old religious system.

I have no resentment against anyone, regret nothing, and am grateful for all who have helped me reach where I am today. I was a Southern Baptist in my beliefs before my inward change. The denomination has flaws just like any other denomination, but I love my Southern Baptist brothers and sisters. I needed to experience everything I did over the last three decades in order to write this book, which I hope will be helpful to others who may be doubting, questioning, and rethinking what they currently believe. No matter how messed up things may seem in your own religious situation, healing and soul restoration are closer than you might think. Keep reading!

Scott Cook
November 2023
Plano, Texas

INTRODUCTION

The Pew Research Center estimates that by 2070 less than fifty percent of the U.S. population will identify as Christian. Less than thirty-five percent will regularly attend a Christian church.

Since the 1990s, large numbers of Americans have left Christianity to join the growing ranks of U.S. adults who describe their religious identity as atheist, agnostic or "nothing in particular." This accelerating trend is reshaping the U.S. religious landscape, leading many people to wonder what the future of religion in America might look like.[1]

This process has been slowly building over the last sixty years. It has reached critical mass in the past ten years due to advancing technology, political divisions, theological deconstruction, and the failure of the current organized church structure and leadership.

Technological innovations such as the internet, cell phones, and social media have changed how people view and interact with religion, denominations, church, and theology. Political divisions have hastened these changes. People who used to meet at church, worship, eat together, and serve Christ no longer do so because of underlying yet palatable political differences. This has accelerated the speed at which church members leave their churches and often leave organized Christianity altogether.

Theological differences have increased into what can only be described as a new reformation.[2] Many Christians, especially younger ones, are no longer willing to accept the evangelical dogma of their parents or grandparents. Some Christians have left their churches and are deconstructing their theology — tearing down what they were taught growing up to its most basic level — and then reconstructing their theology based on the love and compassion of the true person of Jesus Christ, His life, and teaching.

A day doesn't go by that we don't hear of the failures of the current institutional church structure and leadership. From Catholic priests abusing children over the years and leadership covering it up to Southern Baptist ministers abusing their members and then having their crimes covered up by congregational and denominational leadership. Megachurch pastors of all denominations, it seems, are in the news because of sexual misbehavior, toxic leadership, or financial misappropriation. And small churches continue to struggle as a younger generation sees the institutional church as irrelevant to their lives.

But as dreary and depressing as this sounds, I believe institutional churches have played a necessary part for many people. In my own life, it was necessary so that I could come to the end of believing in outward religious organizations and dogma, and begin the process of deconstructing my theology to see the reality of what it means to be a spiritual person in Christ.

I was born, raised, and lived as a Southern Baptist for fifty-two years. I have a master's degree from Southwestern Baptist Theological Seminary in Fort Worth, Texas, and pastored or served vocationally in four different churches. I was theologically conservative and evangelistic, believing in the denomination I was a part of and their doctrinal beliefs regarding the Bible, church, morality, and the necessity of standing for the "truth." The only problem was that I was missing the most important part: love, which has no expectations, conditions, or demands. The kind of love with which God loves us is known as *agape* love. I had no understanding of this love. In time, I would come to experience it and let everything else go so that love in Christ Jesus could be the foundation of my life.

This book is the story of my journey from Christian denominational religion and its dogma to living in the freedom of God's grace, love, and unconditional acceptance in Christ. It is a story of deconstructing my theology to the point of only having the love of God and Jesus Christ. This deconstruction was necessary so God could build the truth of His love for me on top of my theological ruins — unconditional love with no expectations and the reality of my union with Christ that He accomplished before I was born. My story isn't isolated; others have taken this lonely road.

The book is divided into three parts. In Part One, I discuss dying to my religious denominational god and dogma. The first two chapters cover the paradox of religion; promising much, yet delivering very little. And even though it delivered little, I kept returning like an addict, hoping the next hit would take me higher. As the scripture says, "Clouds without rain, wells without water." That was me! I look at the codependency I lived from and the legalistic and fear-based teaching I grew up with; my trying to please everyone and the church organization, yet never really being myself, and how I sacrificed who I was to try to be what religion wanted me to be. Chapter three is about the inevitable crises of belief, the soul pain of living in something I no longer believed, and the physical suffering that ultimately helped me begin to change. Chapter four looks at the process of letting go of control and the despair I felt when I realized how wrong I had been about so many things.

Part Two is about the beginnings of my deconstruction and the neurological illness that sped up that process. Reconstructing the untouchable doctrines and dogma that my denomination did not allow you to touch, and how liberating it was to do that. And finally, the pain and difficulty of leaving my tribe and the inevitable consequences for my relationships, both family and friends.

The last part of the book, looks at the years after I left the organized institutional church. It was at this time I began to reconstruct my theology, so that I now enjoy the reality of a loving God, no longer obligated to denominational theologians, pastors, or church friends to instruct or warn me about "biblical error." Instead, I started to trust God and myself, freeing me to love others just as they are. Finally, and most importantly, was my transition to living an inner life of the spirit that's much more tranquil, restful, and peaceful.

It has been quite a journey and not at all what I expected. If you had told my thirty-something self that I would be writing a book like this, I would have scoffed at you. It is hard to see beyond your theological nose when raised in a religious bubble. The bubble seems secure, solid, and comforting. In some ways, you do not have to think for yourself or consider things very deeply. Just show up to a church building, sing some worship songs, and listen to a motivational message that upholds the theological line, and all is well. Go home, watch the football game, eat lunch, and know you have all the truth about God, the Bible, morality, and how everyone should live — until you do not. Then, in a splendid, incredible moment, it all comes crashing down, and the most painful and wonderful thing has happened: You are no longer sure of anything. And that is the start of the adventure.

PART ONE
DYING TO LIVE

1

THE PARADOX OF CHRISTIAN RELIGION: "CHURCHIANITY"

It is difficult to free fools from the chains they revere.
— Voltaire

The word "religion" is from the old Latin *religare*, meaning to bind, and *religio*, meaning obligation, bond, or reverence. The medieval French word *religion* was originally meant to describe life under the monastic vow: someone bound to a set of practices and beliefs. The word "religion" is defined in the Merriam-Webster Dictionary as "a personal set or institutionalized system of religious attitudes, beliefs, and practices."[1] The Oxford Dictionary defines "religion" as "action or conduct indicating belief in, obedience to, and reverence for a god, gods, or similar superhuman power; the performance of religious rites or observances."[2]

Today, religion in the West has become associated with Christianity, churches, organizations, and institutions that claim to represent God and Jesus Christ on Earth. The Catholic church alone boasts over 1.1 billion adherents to the faith, and Christianity boasts over 2.25 billion. Islam has over a billion followers, and Judaism has over 100 million.

But monotheistic religions do not have a monopoly on the word "religion." Most people consider Hinduism and Buddhism to be religions. The exception would be a practicing Buddhist, as they would disagree with you. They would tell you Buddhism is simply a set of teachings for a higher consciousness of living.

Christianity has churches; Islam has mosques; Judaism has synagogues; and Hinduism has temples. They each have sacred writings, beliefs to adhere to, standards for living, and official and unofficial institutions and organizations. All are built on the following belief: *We are right.* It is no more complex than that. Christians argue Christ's resurrection as proof of the validity of their faith. While Muslims argue the Koran and the Prophet Muhammed. Depending on your flavor of Judaism, you would probably argue that the Jewish scriptures (Torah) were given to Israel through Moses and the covenant given to Abraham by God.

When I use the word religion, I want to be very clear about what I am communicating. I was born and raised in Christianity, so I can only speak from that context. I will leave it to Muslims, Jews, and Hindus to express their unique experience and understanding of their respective religions. I am not critiquing their religious beliefs or attempting to address their unique religious experience in this book

My definition of the Christian religion (or Churchianity, if you will), as used in this book, is as follows: *Human efforts to standardize, codify, control, protect, and proclaim a belief system regarding God the Father, Jesus Christ, His Son, and the Holy Spirit through institutional structures, organizational methods, outward practices, and observances based on cultural affinities.*

LEARNED BELIEFS AND BEHAVIOR

Since my earliest days, I have often wondered, "Why do we put on our finest attire when we go to church?" " Why do we not do the same for the evening service?" These questions were my first conscious taste of religion, signaling that something felt amiss, yet no one seemed willing to discuss it. My parents would explain that we dressed up as a sign of respect to God, but deep down, I knew there had to be more to it than that. Did God truly concern Himself with our Sunday morning wardrobe? And if so, why only in the morning and not the evening? These thoughts filled my young mind, and the answers remained elusive.

We dressed up because that was expected in our unique religious culture. It was in keeping with religious expectations and had nothing to do with Jesus or His message of love and grace. In other words, we learned from parents, fellow members, and religious leaders traditions that had been handed down from their parents and religious leaders. It was Churchianity, a melding of theology, philosophy, traditions, and cultural affinities into something that does not remotely resemble the life, teaching, and unconditional love of Jesus Christ.

The same can be said of the strict, legalistic rules governing our behavior, such as the prohibition on attending R-rated movies (although PG-13 is permissible), abstaining from drinking, smoking, engaging in sexual activity, and avoiding drugs. There were also expectations regarding dating and marrying like-minded believers. I often questioned these rules, thinking, "If the apostle Paul encouraged Timothy to drink when necessary, why can we not?" "People have been smoking for centuries, so why can't we?" Although it was no secret that some churchgoers indulged in a smoke before the service. I never took up smoking, so that was not an issue for me. However, when it came to dating, I was drawn to good-looking girls, even if they were non-believers.

Over time, I saw these prohibitions and outward customs as normal and acceptable. I learned and adjusted my behavior to be accepted in the tribe and to adapt to Churchianity. The same was true for the denominational doctrines. I eventually accepted them without hesitancy and expected the same of others in our community of believers. From cultural demands to religious rules to denominational doctrines,

I embraced them to receive acceptance, love, inclusion, and a place to belong. These were things that gave meaning to my life, order to how I lived, and boundaries for what I could and could not do. It was Churchianity and had nothing to do with who I was in Christ Jesus. These rules, expectations, and dogma were unrelated to the spiritual reality of my life in Christ. They were learned beliefs and behaviors I had learned, and I was eager to let go of them in time.

SURRENDERING YOUR MIND AND LOYALTY

The longer you are under a specific doctrinal teaching, the stronger your allegiance to it becomes. For instance, if you were raised in a church emphasizing a predestination doctrine, your loyalty would naturally be inclined toward that teaching. However, this doctrine may cause moral problems concerning God's character, or it may no longer be as convincing as it once was. Over time, you might move away from it in search of an alternative perspective. This process is common among theologians, although they often do not openly acknowledge it. Nevertheless, those initial teachings will serve as your default theological standpoint.

I was raised in Southern Baptist churches and later became a pastor within that tradition. In these churches, there was a strong emphasis on the concept of free will and the individual's choice to be saved from eternal damnation. That was my theological default setting. Everything I had been taught about these doctrines while growing up still rattled around in my theological brain, coloring how I viewed God, myself, and others. I gave my mind and loyalty to the denominational dogma and the doctrines without realizing I was doing it.

Churchianity demands this price for your inclusion, acceptance, and affection. If you find yourself within this system, you must be willing to embrace the cherished doctrines and dogma it holds dear. It is this demand that gives the religious system its power and influence. However, Jesus did not teach that. He upended the dogma and traditions of religious institutions that claimed to speak for God, a claim still made by many modern churches. His teachings and actions underscored that love, compassion, mercy, gentleness, and empathy hold greater significance than theological doctrines and dogma. The religious leaders of His day killed Him for it.

THE SOUL'S NEVER-ENDING THIRST

Religion fails to satisfy our universal longing: the soul's thirst. It is this relentless thirst (seeking and longing for inner peace and fulfillment) that everyone strives for. Within the Christian religion, there is no remedy for this deep longing other than imposing additional activity, service, class, seminar, retreat, or a list of dos and do nots. It is crucial to grasp that none of these external factors can satiate the inner thirst that resides within us.

In the realm of Churchianity or the Christian religion, the focus often lies outside of oneself. Whether it is reading the Bible, singing worship songs in services, listening to messages, giving, taking on leadership roles, teaching a class or small group, helping in the nursery, working on a committee, witnessing, speaking in tongues, lighting a candle, attending services weekly, performing in Easter or Christmas pageants, or participating in retreats — the list goes on. Even with this wide range of activities, individuals often find themselves left with the same soul thirst they had before participating in them. The root cause of this spiritual dissatisfaction does not lie in the activities themselves but in the external attention and emphasis placed upon them.

Burnout among pastors is at an all-time high, with nearly one-third leaving the ministry within a decade of serving. Pastors are seeking psychological counseling at higher rates than ever before. Why is this happening? The root cause lies in the absence of inner emotional and mental peace that remains unaddressed by external religious activities.

A religious organization that demands time, effort, and financial contributions is, by its very definition, outwardly focused. Pastors are judged based on metrics such as church growth, ministry expansion, construction of larger buildings, and whether the service and messages are dynamic enough. However, none of these factors are essential for a spiritually vibrant life. Everything necessary for an individual's spiritual well-being resides within them through their union with Christ. It does not hinge on church membership, attendance, giving, or specific programs. When our focus shifts toward our union with Christ, soul peace and rest are natural.

> *Jesus said, "Come to me, all you who are weary and burdened, and I will give you rest. Take my yoke on you and learn from me, because I am gentle and humble in heart, and you will find rest for your souls. For my yoke is easy to bear, and my load is not hard to carry."* Matthew 11:28-30 NET

Notice this verse does not mention committees, worship songs, organizational commitments, or sermons. Just come to Jesus, and He will give you rest.

The apostle Paul put it this way, "But whatever gain I had, I counted as loss for the sake of Christ. Indeed, I count everything as loss because of the surpassing worth of knowing Christ Jesus my Lord. For his sake I have suffered the loss of all things and count them as rubbish, in order that I may gain Christ." Philippians 3:7-8 ESV

He lives in you now and always has. His Spirit is eternally intertwined and one with your spirit. There is nothing to do, no destination to reach, and nothing to accomplish. In Him, it is complete. Simply embrace and enjoy your soul's rest and peace, which flows naturally from this union.

It would take fifty-three years for me to begin to enter that rest. Achieving it meant turning my back on the religious community I had been a part of for my entire life — a decision I knew was necessary but had resisted for years. The soul can never find actual rest in outside pursuits, whether religious or secular. I might have paid lip service to this idea in the past, but my actions and priorities told a different story.

Transitioning from the confines of a religious mindset to the expansive freedom of a spiritual one takes time. The unquenched thirst of the soul can serve to propel this transformation. Yet, there must be something more, a catalyst that shatters the theological glass house.

CHURCHIANITY DOESN'T ACTUALLY WORK

As the old saying goes, "Insanity is doing the same thing repeatedly, expecting a different result." Addicts of every kind find themselves trapped in this cycle, perpetually chasing a higher high, constantly yearning for an elusive satisfaction that never truly arrives. Christian religious institutions and those involved in them find themselves in a similar pattern. I, too, found myself entangled in this cycle for over fifty years, clinging to the hope that, somehow, the outcome would change, but it never did. Deep down, I knew these religious activities were not yielding practical results in people's lives. I witnessed the spiritual immaturity and lack of growth, yet my allegiance to doctrine, dogma, and denomination remained steadfast because they represented my tribe and community. However, it was when I faced a neurological illness that my world came crashing down around me — and with it, my commitment to a system that promised so much but delivered so little, consistently keeping people coming back for something that would never satisfy their soul thirst.

As I grew in spiritual revelation and maturity, I noticed something: Doctrine, dogma, and organizations were not growing with me. My theology was changing, but theirs was not. My understanding of spirituality was growing, but theirs was not. And my willingness to get outside my intellectual comfort zone was growing, but theirs was not. I was moving higher, and they were at the same place they had always been: stagnant. And my willingness to get outside my intellectual comfort zone was growing, but theirs could not. I was moving higher, and they were at the same place they had always been: stagnant.

The organization and its members found themselves stuck in a repetitive cycle, hoping for a different outcome, yet it never came. They persisted in their doctrinal, organizational, institutional, and spiritual practices because it was a place of acceptance, loyalty to their tribe, and a comfort zone they were unwilling to leave.

In my book *Alignment of Authentic Love: Living Your Highest Life*, I wrote about the chronic neurological illness that suddenly afflicted me in 2016, causing a rapid weight loss of thirty pounds in forty-five days, impacting my balance and mobility. It also caused persistent headaches, brain fog, and dizziness. I consulted with numerous specialists, including neurologists, rheumatologists, endocrinologists, and alternative medicine physicians. I endured over three hundred blood tests and underwent multiple MRIs, CT scans, and PET scans, all to no avail. No one could give a diagnosis. It would be more than three years before a doctor finally conducted a skin biopsy test, revealing that I had small nerve fiber neuropathy. While some treatments can alleviate the pain, no medical solution for complete healing exists.

Although not from God, this illness helped open my eyes to the reality of a good God who is Love and has always loved me perfectly. In the midst of suffering, I realized for the first time that my religious beliefs about God, Jesus, the material universe, the Bible, and the organizations and structures claiming to follow and represent Him on Earth were limited, biased, and, at times, outright wrong.

Suffering can strip away our reliance on religious ideas, dogma, institutions, and leaders, leaving only Christ (the Divine Source, the Light) as our identity. All the doctrines, sermons, beliefs, and rules that once held me crumbled. In that moment, only God, as unconditional love revealed in Christ, who embodies Love in human form, became the sole focus. All my efforts and theological certainties vanished, leaving me in a state of surrender.

What truly matters above all else is God's unwavering, unconditional love. Everything that I, and many others, had placed our faith in and relied upon turned out to be a mirage. None of it was real because it could not lead us to the reality of God's unconditional love, which has no expectations. None of it allowed us to dwell in a state of perpetual soul rest and peace because of His boundless love. Only God's love brings healing. His love that softens and turns a hardened heart, healing the emotional wounds of the past. His unconditional love had begun its transformative work in me. I was now utterly convinced religious doctrines are not essential or of primary importance.

This point marked only the beginning of my journey. To break free and rebuild would require confronting one of my religious demons: people-pleasing!

2

RELIGIOUS CODEPENDENCY

I surrendered myself to the cages of others' expectations, cultural mandates and institutional allegiances. Until I buried who I was in order to become what I should be. I lost myself when I learned how to please.[1]
Glennon Doyle

As a conservative evangelical pastor, expressing skepticism about the existence of Hell, could lead your congregation and denomination to seriously question your suitability for continuing in your pastoral role.

Take, for instance, Rob Bell, the former Mars Hill Bible Church pastor in Grandville, Michigan. He authored a book titled *Love Wins*, highlighting God's encompassing love for all people and presenting a more nuanced interpretation of Hell than traditionally held in evangelical theology.

"In the end, "Love Wins" did turn out to be a kind of farewell. The members of Mars Hill found themselves having to answer for their membership in a church that was suddenly notorious. Eventually, Bell decided that it would be best for everyone if he left the church he had founded. In September, half a year after the publication of "Love Wins," he told the congregation that he would be stepping down."[2]

Despite his intellectual honesty and theological transparency, these views led to his resignation from the church he founded. Furthermore, he faced relentless criticism from the evangelical religious establishment.

Today, he is a prominent author and speaker dedicated to deconstructing Christian theology and rethinking spirituality. In doing so, he broke free from the confines of religious conformity and people-pleasing.

Each Christian church shares a common trait: a gathering place for people-pleasers. Within these religious communities, Christians often learn to survive in the religious structure by mastering the art of pleasing others. This inclination is not limited to religious circles; it is a common thread in various social settings, including relationships, families, corporate environments, and governmental structures. However, religious institutions possess a distinctive feature: unyielding theological belief systems and rigid institutional structures. Within these realms, conformity to established doctrines and norms is encouraged and often deemed vital for long-term inclusion and acceptance in the religious community.

CHRISTIAN RELIGION AND PEOPLE-PLEASING

Several years out of seminary, I started to doubt the religious system I was a part of and questioned the effectiveness and relevance of what we taught in people's everyday lives. Furthermore, I felt a sense of powerlessness and impotence in my personal walk with Christ. I began to read more about the Holy Spirit and our exchanged life in Christ.

Gradually, my perspective on grace shifted. I re-evaluated key tenets of my faith, such as the nature of grace, the Holy Spirit's role in a believer's life, the full implications of Christ's finished work, and the true meaning of living by faith. This shift in belief brought with it a sense of trepidation. I hesitated to share my evolving theological views, fearing rejection and misunderstanding from my peers and congregation. My role at a large church compounded these fears. I worried that openly discussing my changing perspectives might jeopardize my position, especially since these views were beginning to diverge significantly from the church's established doctrines.

Some members of the church who met weekly to discuss these theological changes, gradually shifted their beliefs. Yet, like me, in the broader context of the church, they were an extreme minority.

This new way of thinking left me feeling like a fish out of water, like an outsider looking in and no longer a part of the whole. My tendency to be a people-pleaser was still dominant at this point in my spiritual walk, creating an internal conflict. I suppressed my true thoughts and conformed to the expectations of my pastor, fellow staff, and the church leadership. I maintained the peace by staying silent and toeing the line, but it was at the cost of my authenticity.

Like many religions, Christianity encompasses a variety of statements of faith and beliefs that its followers generally accept and strive to live by. Within its institutions, hierarchical structures are common, and some may display patriarchal, misogynistic, and exclusionary tendencies.

Typically, those institutions are led by senior pastors who hold significant power and control, with the extent varying based on the specific context and congregation. Supporting them are elders, often men, who contribute to the administration of various ministries and the oversight of congregational activities. Further contributing to church life are deacons and lay members, who assist with ministry needs and sometimes lead or teach. Lay committees are usually responsible for managing the church's overall administration. Each church is frequently affiliated with a larger denominational body, examples being the Southern Baptist Convention, Assemblies of God, or Church of Christ.

In this environment, many individuals work diligently to avoid "coloring outside the theological lines," endeavoring to remain in the good graces of other members and the church leadership. Pastors often find themselves trying to please their congregation and the staff members trying to please the pastor. Congregation members, in turn, attempt to steer clear of sin and engage in "good" deeds, all to gain the approval of both the pastor and their fellow churchgoers. The church system overall is trying to be successful and thus satisfy the congregation and the denomination. So, everyone puts on a mask, comes to church, and performs.

In some religious environments, there is an unspoken expectation to unconditionally accept established beliefs and norms — to "check your brain in at the door." In such settings, asking challenging questions, disagreeing with sacred theological tenets, or committing certain acts deemed "sins" can swiftly lead to disapproval or conflict.

Growing up as a Southern Baptist, I was ingrained with the importance of seeking approval and fitting in from an early age. Church was more than a place of worship; it was the social hub of my life, where friendships were forged and a sense of community was nurtured — it was my tribe. I quickly learned not to offend or "cause division" within the body. This unwritten rule, emphasizing harmony and conformity, subtly kept us all in check, influencing how we interacted within our community.

For example, during my high school years, the social dynamics of our youth group were such that if I dated someone, it was not long before the whole group found out. Crucial to this was the question of my date's religious background. If she was not from our church, which church did she attend? Was it deemed acceptable by our standards? If she was not a Christian, I was going against tribal rules and would lose the approval of my church peers, youth minister, Sunday school teacher, and others.

Consequently, I often made choices in my dating life that were less about personal preference and more about gaining approval from my church community. Instead of pursuing relationships with the girls I was genuinely interested in, I chose those I knew would be well-received by church members. I learned the skill of people-pleasing early on within the church environment. It became a habitual response that I honed effectively, often at the expense of my desires and individuality.

FAMILY PRESSURE

In addition to church pressures, I also faced expectations from my family to be a "good" Christian and tow the party line regarding the church and theology. My natural disposition leans towards cynicism; I have always approached things and people with a degree of mistrust, often asking questions until I find understandable and convincing answers. However, questions and doubts about our faith, the Bible, or denomination were not encouraged in our household. The norm was a straightforward acceptance: The pastor said it; the church believes it; we believe it, and so should you. This family dynamic added another layer of complexity to my spiritual journey, as it often put my inherent questioning nature at odds with the unspoken rule of absolute belief.

Therefore, it became easier to accept what the spiritual leaders told me rather than constantly questioning everything and forming my own conclusions based on personal beliefs. Through this path of least resistance with my parents, I gained their acceptance by accepting the church dogma rather than expressing my opinions and having an honest debate about the theological, doctrinal, or denominational belief or stance.

Every family or tribe, including religious organizations, is bound together by its own myths, stories, and tales of the past. These narratives are more than just folklore; they form the cornerstone of a group's belief system, allowing cohesiveness, its members' protection, and unity. However, when someone within the group begins to question or challenge these shared myths and stories, it creates a rift within the tribe, disrupting the group's unity. If not dealt with, it may even influence or unsettle others within the tribe.

As a teenager, my brother became interested in meditation. This concept was taboo in our religious circle at the time. To us, "meditation" was a word loaded with negative connotations, suggesting deception by the "enemy" (Satan). My brother Darrell's interest in meditation was part of a broader journey of doubting and questioning what he had learned in church, exploring different ideas and practices.

Today, meditation is commonplace and a widely accepted practice for its health benefits. Many Christians use meditation, and we help teach clients to meditate in the spiritual counseling ministry I founded. But in those days, it was viewed with suspicion.

Concerned, my parents asked the pastor to speak with Darrell and warn him about the perceived dangers of meditation. As they explained these dangers, Darrell later shared with me his realization, "This was not my circus, and these were not my monkeys." He no longer identified with the tribe or revered these pastors as my parents did. Fortunately for him, people-pleasing was less of a problem than it was for me, allowing him a different perspective on our faith and practices.

RELIGIOUS CODEPENDENTS

"Codependency" is defined in the Merriam-Webster Dictionary as "a psychological condition or a relationship in which a person manifesting low self-esteem and a strong desire for approval has an unhealthy attachment to another often controlling or manipulative person (such as a person with an addiction to alcohol or drugs)."[3] In my case, the "controlling and manipulative person" was not an individual but the entity of the religion itself. I found myself in the grips of this entity, where my need for approval and low self-esteem led to an unhealthy and codependent relationship with religious doctrines and expectations.

From a young age, I was taught to believe something was inherently wrong with me. The doctrine that I was a "fallen" person, a sinner by nature and not merely by action, was a constant refrain in my upbringing — a notion that still makes my stomach churn. This message was not just from one source; it came from those I admired most: my parents, religious leaders, and other respected figures in the community. The cumulative effect of hearing from these authoritative voices is that you tend to believe them. To say that I had low self-esteem is an understatement. From my earliest memories, the message was clear and unrelenting: "Something is wrong with you." This relentless narrative shaped my self-perception.

The teachings I received regularly painted a troubling paradox. I was taught that God cannot love me for who I am. His presence cannot tolerate me in my natural state, and direct communication with me, as I am, is out of the question. The message was clear: There is something inherently wrong with me. Moreover, this doctrine implied that God created me with these flaws only to potentially reject and condemn me to Hell one day.

On the other hand, there was the message of His love: that Jesus died for my sins as a sacrifice to save me from the very fate that my "deficiencies" warranted. This meant that not only was I inherently deficient and unacceptable, but also that my existence necessitated the death of someone else.

The layers of guilt, shame, and self-degradation that stemmed from trying to reconcile these conflicting messages were overwhelming and hard to articulate.

Due to my struggle with low self-esteem, seeking acceptance from God and those around me became the focus of my life. The approval of my parents, especially my mother, as her acceptance was rare, was a constant goal. My quest for acceptance extended to friends, teachers, and neighbors, who, I now realize, were likely struggling with their own self-worth issues. I tirelessly sought the approval of people at church and religious leaders who appeared to have everything in order and seemed far "better" than me.

But above all, I yearned for God's acceptance. I longed for Him to look down, see my efforts, and feel a momentary sense of pride in me, even if just briefly — at least enough to feel like I was not a complete failure or a waste of time. At the very least, I clung to the hope that perhaps He would find me acceptable enough to spare me from the fate of Hell.

By its very nature, Churchianity demands that you seek the approval of those in your religious tribe, the very group responsible for defining the rules and administering consequences if anyone gets out of line. In this way, it robs you of your soul and the person you were created to be, the authentic you who may not fit into the mold that religion demands.

DENYING MY AUTHENTIC SELF

In my denomination, acceptance within the religious establishment and the church community required me to adopt the belief that I was inherently flawed, a "sinner" from birth, and to embrace this as my core identity. This also meant acknowledging that all people were sinners. However, to do that implied a denial of any inherent goodness within us. To accept this religious tenant meant denying something deep within myself, something I was created to be but now felt unsafe and unworthy to be: my authentic self. It became a challenge to simply be myself because God or the church community did not accept the true me.

Who is your authentic self? This question was explored in my earlier book, *The Alignment of Authentic Love: Living Your Highest Life.* Your authentic self is not the person you think you aspire to become. Instead, it is the person God has always known you to be in union with Christ Jesus. It encompasses your soul, which is the mind, will, and emotions. Your authentic self is the person you were created to be — whether black, white, or brown, male or female, introverted or extroverted, people-oriented or task-oriented, left-brained or right-brained, adventurous or cautious, aesthetically inclined or volitionally motivated. In a world of billions of people, each person is unique and one-of-a-kind.

Your spirit is the essence of who you are and interacts with your soul perfectly. Unfortunately, the soul often bears the scars of traumas, hurts, and disappointments, erecting emotional and mental barriers between itself and the spirit. Instead of loving yourself, these experiences can lead to the formation of false identities rooted in these past wounds. For instance, when someone says, "You were born a sinner, and you sin because that is your identity," it is spiritual abuse, inflicting emotional wounds and establishing the false identity: "There is something wrong with me."

As this false identity takes hold, individuals may eventually behave in accordance with it, as our beliefs shape our actions. Over time, the authentic self becomes suppressed, and people don masks, pretending that everything is perfect in their Christian life, family, and more, all in a quest for the approval of their religious peers.

In Christ, there is not, nor has there ever been, anything wrong with us. God loves us just as we are. No corrections or adjustments are needed. We were created in His image and likeness, and that is enough. But a steady diet of "You are a sinner by nature" and "You deserve Hell"[4] creates a false mindset that fights against the truth of the union we have with God in Christ.

In my case, the tools of control and fear employed by the Christian institution had taken their toll. Instead of loving my authentic self, I despised who I genuinely was. Rather than embracing my inherent identity, I rejected my authentic self. I began to try to change myself into what I believed would make me a "better" person who would be "included" in the church community and assured of a "place" in Heaven.

If I recited the prayer with sincerity, asking God to forgive me as a sinner in need of a savior, then God would save me from Hell and remove His anger toward me because of all my sins. However, no matter how dedicated I was to praying, faithfully attending church, giving offerings, reading the Bible, and eventually even becoming a pastor, the haunting thought persisted: "There is something wrong with me, and I will forever be a disappointment to God."

Manipulation, fear, and control are all tactics wielded in the name of Christian religious dogma and institutional power. Unfortunately, many individuals within these institutions have never been taught to love themselves or encouraged to explore perspectives beyond their narrow theological prism.

FINDING MY AUTHENTIC SELF

The neurological illness I experienced became the catalyst for a profound crisis of faith, which, in turn, heightened my awareness of my religious people-pleasing. I spent over two years trying to find out what was wrong with my body. The uncertainty and not knowing caused me to feel vulnerable, weak, and depressed.

Yet, during this period of immense physical and emotional upheaval, I found myself re-evaluating every facet of my belief system that I had held so tightly. Existential questions consumed my thoughts — Why am I going through this illness if God was a good God of love? Why have I lost my career, ability to earn an income, health, financial stability, and purpose for living?

As I grappled with these questions, I found myself interrogating every other belief I held. By the time I was done tearing down my theological house of cards, all that was left was Jesus. And I had doubts about Him.

This brought me to a place of desperation with more questions than answers. I was no longer mentally closed off to truth outside my denomination and small Christian religious circle that had held me like a prison. I was doubting everything and open to everything. This pivotal moment was necessary for my liberation from the confines of the Christian religion, allowing me to embrace true spirituality and my authentic self in Christ. I was being freed from a theological prison that I thought was a home, a denominational tradition that I thought was a firm foundation, and from Christian institutionalism that I thought was the church on Earth. None of those things were true.

Do not misunderstand me. I wholeheartedly support believers coming together as a family, united in Christ, to love each other and share the message of God's love and our union with Him in Christ. However, it is essential to distinguish this genuine purpose from what has evolved within institutional Christianity over the past two millennia. Modern institutional Christianity often emphasizes material concerns, external organizational structures, doctrinal purity, theological dogma, and a performance-oriented mindset, whether in worship services or personal conduct. The original purpose of the early believers was about embracing God's love in Christ Jesus and the simplicity of following Him in spirit.

The freedom that accompanied my acceptance of my authentic self, with all its flaws, past failures, present struggles, and uncertainties, was genuinely liberating. God was love, and everything else had to take a back seat to that enormous conclusion. It allowed me to let go of the constant need to please others, whether it was my family, the church, friends, or even myself, as I had been my harshest critic.

Each day had previously been a relentless cycle of self-criticism, berating myself for falling short, not living up to perceived standards of holiness, or not working hard enough. It felt like I was perpetually letting down God and everyone else. However, discovering my true self in Him, one with Christ, liberated me from the performance trap.

This realization allowed me to breathe, accept myself fully, and savor each moment without the burden of relentless self-judgment. My authentic self is spiritually in Christ and has always been because nothing is outside Christ. Nothing.

Codependency is as addictive as heroin, fentanyl, and alcohol. In some ways, people in religious circles are trapped in addiction, not just a system. The leaders are often narcissistic and attract people-pleasers who support the system and supply them with new converts to follow and please. It can be an unending circle you never find your way out of. Most do not.

The extreme emotional and mental distress that accompanies the realization that many of your cherished beliefs were flawed and that the organizations and institutions you placed your trust in do not align with what you believe or what Jesus intended can be incredibly overwhelming. However, it is essential to understand that this pain serves a purpose — it paves the way for spiritual freedom and a life of inner rest and peace where you experience your spiritual inheritance.

3

THE SUFFERING OF ENLIGHTENMENT

Never let a good crisis go to waste.
Winston Churchill

The heresy of Galileo was a disagreement between the Italian astronomer Galileo Galilei and the Roman Catholic Church in the early 17th century. Galileo supported the idea that the earth rotates around the sun, known as the heliocentric theory. On the other hand, the church supported the geocentric theory, which claimed that the sun and other celestial bodies revolve around the earth.

At that time, the church had significant power and influence, and they believed that the heliocentric theory contradicted the Bible, which they considered the ultimate source of truth. Therefore, Galileo's support for the heliocentric theory threatened the church's authority and interpretation of scripture.

The church condemned Galileo's theory as heretical, which means they considered it against the church's teachings and view of scripture. They also ordered him to abandon his support for the theory and prohibited him from teaching or writing about it. Consequently, Galileo spent the last nine years of his life under house arrest.

Despite the church's initial condemnation and ill-treatment of Galileo's heliocentric theory, it gradually gained acceptance, bolstered by the contributions of scientists like Johannes Kepler and Isaac Newton. By the mid-18th century, the church had lifted its ban on books supporting the heliocentric theory. Finally, in a significant turn in 1992, the church officially acknowledged that they had erred in their treatment of Galileo, and Pope John Paul II expressed regret for the church's actions.

Galileo was right, yet he suffered for believing something that clashed with official church doctrine. Such enlightenment often entails some form of suffering. My own journey, transitioning from my tribe's specific religious beliefs to embracing the unconditional love of God and a renewed interpretation of scripture, was both essential and arduous. It exacted a heavy toll on Galileo, and I discovered it would also demand a significant price from me.

CRISIS OF PHYSICAL SUFFERING

Navigating a crisis often brings about perspectives that might remain undiscovered in its absence. Life-altering events like the death of a loved one, financial troubles, divorce, or health decline are such crises. My own experience began with a chronic neurological illness that cost me my health, followed by the loss of my career due to daily functional impairments. This led to anger toward God for permitting the disease and frustration over losing my health, job, and family's financial security. Yet, this very crisis initiated the dismantling of the theological constructs I had been inhabiting.

During my physical ordeal, I started questioning my beliefs about God, re-evaluating my understanding of Him, and scrutinizing the theological tenets I had long embraced.

In response to my questions, He seemed to have two questions for me: The first was, "Do you believe I am perfect love and that I have always loved you perfectly?" The second question naturally followed: "If you believe I am perfect love, would you be willing to trust Me?"

For more than two years, I grappled with those two questions. Honestly, I struggled to see Him as a God of love or as one who could be trusted.

Everything became subject to question, not just my theological beliefs but also my denominational allegiances, the divinity of Christ, the reality of Hell, the notion of God as Love (a concept I had never accepted), the idea of salvation from an angry God, the true meaning of atonement, and the authenticity of the Bible's claims. The more the illness worsened, the more questions I had.

CRISES OF FAITH

I came to a proper understanding of faith by losing my faith altogether.

My questions far outnumbered the answers I had:

- How could I trust a God I had shared with others, preached about, worked for, and strived to please to allow such adversity to befall me?
- How could He stand by as I lost my career and ability to earn a living?
- Is He truly a God of love or one of vindictive punishment, deriving pleasure from watching His creations suffer, only to cast them into eternal fire for not reciting the "sinner's prayer" and declaring undying devotion to Him?
- Does He genuinely exist, or is He merely a figment of our collective imagination, born from myths perpetuated across countless millennia?

The crises of faith I experienced served as a catalyst, enabling me to let go of what was unnecessary and embrace what truly mattered. In my journey, this meant releasing nearly all the theological teachings I had received, including the deeply ingrained fear of an angry God.

The Bible emphasizes the importance of living by the faith of Christ. For many years, I did not understand what faith was. However, I have since come to understand what genuine faith truly means. I have learned that faith is not about trying to believe in God amidst hardships. Instead, faith is simply seeing that in Christ, whatever is needed has already been accomplished. It is Christ's faithfulness, not my own, that matters to God.

Galatians 2:20 states,

> "I am crucified with Christ: nevertheless I live; yet not I, but Christ liveth in me: and the life which I now live in the flesh I live by the faith of the Son of God, who loved me, and gave himself for me." KJV

The rendering of this verse in the KJV translates it most accurately. It is not our faith *in* Christ but Christ's faith. Faith is seeing the faithfulness of Jesus Christ in His finished work at the cross and resurrection, completed on behalf of every person, and simply agreeing with Him that it is done.

> "Faith assures us of things we expect and convinces us of the existence of things we cannot see." Hebrews 11:1 GW

According to the author of Hebrews, "faith" is defined as the expectation of receiving, coupled with the capacity to perceive the intangible as though it were tangible and presently real.

I like these two explanations.

> Faith believes those things that are not as though they were because, with God, they are. ~ Manley Beasley

> Faith is believing what God believes and saying what
> God says about any matter. ~ Scott Cook

This correct understanding of faith is necessary if we want to have faith that makes a difference to ourselves and others.

In losing everything, I became receptive to what truly mattered: Love. Understanding that God is Love above all else, I realized that the Person of Christ is not a religion. He is not bound to any particular theology, organization, or institution of humanity, nor monopolized by any. Christ embodies agape love, inspiring trust, peace, and rest in one's inner being. This love is unconditional, without expectations, and never vindictive. I realized I could trust in God's love for me in the present moment, even when everything happening in my life was telling me I could not. If I could believe in His unconditional love for me, then I could trust Him in everything and be assured of His eternal love, regardless of the situation.

CRISIS OF THE SOUL

As I navigated this crisis, I found myself resisting changes in my thoughts and emotions. It was challenging to alter my perception of God from a figure of fear and judgment to a loving Father who cares for my well-being and loves me regardless of my failings.

Daily, I grappled with the question: Could God truly be that good? Were these aspects not equally crucial? It seemed unrealistic to think that He would overlook the willful sins of humanity without any form of judgment. The notion that He could be a deity of unconditional love, free of expectations, felt almost blasphemous. I feared divine retribution for even entertaining such thoughts. This period marked a profound crisis of the soul for me, as it put to test every belief I had held about the Creator of the universe and myself.

Crises of the soul arise when our convictions falter, leaving us uncertain about our beliefs and feelings toward them. Such crises disrupt our anchors, leaving us disoriented, unable to discern up from down, right from left, or even the direction of our next step. Religion often thrives on certainty, insisting on acceptance from its followers and imposing its beliefs on the community. In this phase, I stepped away from the conventional definition of a "believer" as defined by religion. I was engulfed in doubt, withholding trust from everyone and everything. Yet, despite its discomfort, this skepticism and uncertainty is a crucial and healthy stage in one's spiritual journey.

Having been deeply ingrained in the evangelical sphere, I was so thoroughly indoctrinated, even to the point of what could be described as brainwashed, that any idea challenging my compact, secure theological beliefs would send me into a state of fear. Fear of being misled, fear of what God might think, or what actions He might take against me. As these challenges intensified and gained momentum, they led me into a spiral of depression, anger, and anxiety. There was a period when even reading the Bible felt unbearable, as it appeared to be filled with nothing but judgment, criticism, and condemnation. My mind and emotions were in turmoil, racing incessantly, and no remedy seemed to slow them down. Doubts, fears, worries, and questions overwhelmed me, interfering even with my ability to sleep.

Yet, during this turmoil, thoughts persisted: What if God is better than I ever imagined? What if my theology needs to be corrected? What if "God is Love" is the only thing that matters? These considerations eventually drew me out of my spiritual crisis and into the reality of a good and loving God who loves me — and even likes me — just as I am. Over time, these new perspectives began to reshape my thoughts and emotions.

CRISES OF REJECTION

When an evangelical faces a crisis of belief, it is often unwise to discuss these doubts with fellow church members. The congregation, or "tribe," typically struggles to comprehend such things. I was acutely aware that pursuing this path of theological deconstruction would come at a cost.

When I shared my doubts about the existence of Hell with my wife, it was initially distressing for her. She reacted with visible upset, finding it hard to grasp my perspective. However, to her credit, she remained open to hearing me out and thoughtfully considered my viewpoints. The concept of Hell holds significant theological importance for Southern Baptists and evangelicals broadly, ranking arguably among their top three doctrinal beliefs.

- Without Hell, why did Jesus need to come and die?
- Without Hell, why should people behave and clean their act up?
- Without Hell, why are we sending missionaries throughout the world?
- Without Hell, why witness to anyone?

All great questions. *And all the wrong questions.*

A better question may be: "If God is first and foremost unconditional, sacrificial love that sets no preconditions and has no expectations, can we honestly say we understand the concept of Hell, or its supposed necessity?" This question marked a pivotal point in my journey of theological deconstruction.

Initially, I shared my growing concerns and doubts with only a few people, treading cautiously. However, as time passed, I gained confidence and became bolder about my changing beliefs. This shift led to resistance from friends at church and others who couldn't comprehend this change in my life. I started experiencing rejection, a particularly challenging experience for someone recovering from codependency. It felt like facing an old adversary, unbidden yet unavoidable. Despite the rejection, social media attacks, and gossip, I knew I could not halt my journey. Regardless of the opposition, the only viable option was to persevere and take the next step.

Eventually, we decided to leave our church, seeking a new spiritual home more aligned with the theological shifts within me. Departing from beloved friends was difficult but necessary. The road less traveled, by necessity, is a lonely one. It would have been simpler to stay silent and remain in familiar surroundings, but that was not an option for me. My nature compelled me to be authentic and heed the Spirit, leading me from the safety of the theological shoreline into the deeper waters of uncertainty, doubt, and endless questions. Living with questions and uncertainty was preferable to clinging to theological certainties and answers that didn't resonate with the truth of God's love.

THE BLINDING LIGHT OF LOVE

As I progressed on this journey of enlightenment, the light of God's love grew brighter in my heart and spirit. The more I questioned everything, the more freedom I found to be myself and enjoy His unconditional love. However, this path came with a cost. The more I embraced questioning everything I had been taught and lived in liberty, the more I felt a withdrawal and even hostility from fellow Christians who challenged and criticized my evolving theology.

During a discussion in my study group, one member suggested exploring a holiness book. At that time, as I immersed myself in the reality of my life in Christ and pursued theological deconstruction, I responded, "There's no need to study a book on holiness. Simply look at yourself in the mirror, and you'll see all the holiness you need to see in Christ." My comment, though true to my understanding, was met with confusion. He was still entrenched in the "I'm a sinner saved by grace" mindset and could not grasp the idea of viewing oneself as inherently holy. While what I said was true, this response did not align with my friend's beliefs, and he struggled to understand my perspective of already being a "holy person."

As love firmly took root in my heart, mind, and emotions — emanating from my inner spirit — I found the freedom to be myself. This love is a bright light, piercing through the darkness and confusion of the mind, ushering in heightened understanding and awareness. It continues to shine ever brighter, filling every shadowed corner with its brightness.

Beliefs and doctrines that once seemed crucial faded into insignificance, their weighty chains broken. Relationships transformed, centering on love rather than mere acceptance. A deep, genuine peace of the soul emerged, transcending mere words. This love brought inner healing, health, and recovery from past toxic beliefs, relationships, and religious associations. It realigned the mind to its true center in Christ, no longer wandering in search of direction but secure in the knowledge that the Direction lives within me.

I am no longer hoping to arrive, but I see in Him that I arrived long before I was born. This light creates confidence to be myself, believe in myself, and be confident in my union with Christ.

4

THE CALL TO SPIRITUAL FREEDOM

Some of us think holding on makes us strong; but sometimes it is letting go.
Hermann Hesse

In Francois du Toit's *Divine Embrace*, there is a moving story about a black eagle living in a cage in the Pretoria Zoo in South Africa for ten years. This eagle spent a decade in captivity and was finally released into the wild. However, when given the chance to fly, it hesitated until it heard the call of another eagle, a call of freedom to soar.

Immediately upon hearing this call, the zoo eagle took flight, breaking free from its cage. It bravely took flight into the unknown, rising to heights it had never experienced, soaring gracefully on the winds as an eagle should.

This was my experience. I heard the call of my true identity in Christ, the unconditional love of a good God, and my soul's deep yearning to soar. The call for spiritual freedom resounded within, and despite the pain, confusion, hurt, and mental stress, I could not turn back. I had to venture into the unknown, ascending on spiritual wings to uncharted heights. Staying where I was simply was no longer possible. But this choice meant embracing some difficult truths.

THE WONDERFUL DESPAIR OF BEING WRONG

It was overwhelming to confront potential theological misconceptions. Could I have been mistaken about God's nature, the concept of eternal Hell, the judgment of "unbelievers," or the idea of penal substitutionary atonement? How could I have held onto these doctrines as the core of my belief system for so long if they might be incorrect? With this reality came despair — the despair of being wrong.

The fear of being so wrong stemmed from pride. I took immense pride in my deeply held theological tenets and beliefs. Above all, I found my greatest source of pride in firmly believing that my denominational tribe held the ultimate truth. This pride was fueled by the fear that if I were mistaken about one thing, what other beliefs might crumble? It felt like a fragile house of cards, poised on the edge of collapse.

Additionally, I feared how all of this would impact my marriage, family, friendships, church life, and reputation. Was I willing to jeopardize the strong relationships I had painstakingly cultivated with those who remained steadfast in their adherence to religious doctrines I no longer embraced? And was I prepared to let go of them?

While teaching an adult Bible study group, I asked: "Would you be willing to consider the possibility that your theological beliefs might be wrong?" Surprisingly, no one was willing to admit potential errors in their understanding of the Bible, Jesus, salvation, the atonement, and Hell. This is a concerning trend within the Christian religion, where fear and pride have become so dominant as to prevent even the possibility of being wrong.

A call for spiritual freedom emerged in this despair of the possibility of being wrong. This freedom brought with it a willingness to consider other viewpoints, to listen to new voices, and to re-examine theological positions I had once hastily dismissed as heretical. In this newfound liberty, fear was no longer the driving force. Instead, it was replaced by a compelling desire to move beyond the status quo, recognizing that this was the only path forward.

ADJUSTING TO THE LIGHT

I was staying at a friend's house in the countryside, where the only external light came from a streetlamp they had installed on a pole at the end of their long gravel driveway. As I turned off my bedside lamp to sleep, the room plunged into intense darkness, and I could not even see my hand in front of my face. A few minutes later, needing to find my way to the door, I turned the lamp back on. The sudden brightness was overwhelming, forcing me to shield my eyes with my hands. Adjusted to the dark, my eyes perceived the light as exceptionally bright for a brief moment. This moment mirrored my spiritual journey: Introducing what seemed like new truths — in reality, centuries-old ideas — into the darkness of my theological "prison cell" was as jarring and illuminating as that sudden light.

In many aspects, the Christian religion keeps its followers within a theological and doctrinal "dark room." Individuals are often restricted to only accepting and knowing what is deemed acceptable by religious authorities. Fear becomes the primary tool to enforce this conformity — fear of doctrinal error, divine wrath, Hell, loss of salvation, disapproval from religious leaders, and ostracization within one's religious tribe. It can be overwhelming when light enters the dark room of theological control and stagnation.

As I began to deconstruct my understanding of who God is, it was like a light being switched on in a dark room. Much like the experience with the bedside table lamp, this revelation (or recently discovered freedom) was initially blinding to me. However, for others who already embraced and knew this unconditional love, it guided their path and warmed their hearts.

Initially, the idea of God as unconditional love was a concept that lay far beyond the boundaries of my theological comfort zone. This new perspective made me feel emotionally unsettled and vulnerable. However, the longer I looked into this light of Love and the reality of God's true character and nature, the more my spiritual vision adjusted to this enlightening truth. My fear of God began to dissolve, giving way to a relationship built on *mutual respect* and love with the Source of all life. No longer clouded by fear, apprehension, and condemnation, I could now see the One who loved me.

CONTROL IS COMFORTING

Control freaks often make terrible car passengers, and I found myself in this precise situation while riding with my younger son. I caught myself instructing him when to turn and what to watch for. I immediately became aware of my behavior and promptly apologized. As I embraced the call to spiritual freedom, I noticed something unsettling: I was losing control of my theological "steering wheel." The structures and beliefs I had relied on to keep my life orderly and predictable were unraveling. Yet, in this process, I recognized that none of what I was losing was essential — my enjoyment came more from the sense of control than the elements themselves.

The Bible is remarkable, offering a wealth of insights if read from a spiritual perspective. However, interpreting it in a strictly literal, materialistic, and rule-based manner can turn it into an instrument for control in the hands of those with a religiously codependent mindset. Such codependents, driven by a deep-seated need for control, believe they can prevent "bad" things from happening to themselves and others and manage chaos. Historically, the church has focused heavily on controlling people's beliefs, thereby losing sight of the only thing that mattered: that all humanity is in Christ Jesus, and Christ is in all of humanity. Jesus' desire was love, not control.

As my theology began to undergo dramatic changes, I became aware of the potential strain or even severing in my relationships with friends and family. The sense of vulnerability, loss, and uncertainty was tangible and even overwhelming at times. The most significant change was the loss of control — a control once firmly anchored in religious doctrine. This control allowed me certainty in my beliefs about God, Jesus, people, and morality. I used the Bible to support my conservative evangelical views — it was my lifeblood. I had definitive answers for every moral question: *Women as preachers? Absolutely not! Gay and Lesbian individuals? Lost and destined for Hell. Women who have abortions? The same fate of Hell awaited them as only evil people would partake in such an act. The wicked who rejected Christ were bound for Hell, while Heaven awaited the repentant and believing.* On and on, I had an answer for everything — until I did not.

This loss of control was unraveling the very fabric of my soul, altering my direction, and reshaping my sense of identity. Suddenly, losing control and not having all the answers became my new normal. Yet, this relinquishing of control was necessary for the spiritual freedom I was experiencing. For the first time in my life, I was venturing into a realm of spiritual liberation, a journey that promised to continue unfolding in the days ahead.

LOVE OR LAW

At the core of my spiritual journey was the ultimate question: Would I choose to live in the light of God's unconditional love that dwells in me or to continue to cling to the rigid, religious dichotomy of dos and do nots, rights and wrongs? Observing the Christian religion, I noticed that despite its teachings about grace, the emphasis often shifted to performance when the rubber hit the road.

Will I live my life based on external markers — people's beliefs, the company they keep, their political or religious affiliations, or adherence to conservative values? Or will I move beyond the confines of organized religion and its systematic rules, instead embracing my true self in Christ — the person I have always been, loved, accepted, adored, and included in Him?

Will I find rest in the completeness of Christ's finished work, or will I continue to strive, trying to add to it through my own actions, decisions, and efforts? Ultimately, will I align myself with the One who is unconditional Love, who loves everyone just as they are, without expectations? Or will I adhere to a law-based system that judges and excludes, condemning those who do not recite a "sinner's prayer." Endorsing misogyny, and ostracizing others — including fellow Christians with differing beliefs — a system that accepts the idea of an eternal Hell, contradictory to the God who asks us to forgive unconditionally yet appears unwilling to do the same?

I chose Love. My heart and soul could no longer resist the call for the spiritual freedom found in the extreme, unconditional agape of a good God. This Love ushers one into inner rest and peace of soul, seeing no one as lesser, excluded, cast out, unworthy, or not good enough. Agape love does not keep a tally of wrongs but instead believes all things, hopes all things, and endures all things. Love never fails, not even throughout eternity — it is forever.

What is greater than love? Whatever your answer, consider it carefully: Do you genuinely believe it, or are you merely echoing what you have been taught over the years?

SOARING

Much like the black eagle in François du Toit's book, which heard the call to embrace its true identity and soar above the hills and mountains, I, too, heard a spiritual call to freedom. This call beckoned me to be my true self in Christ, urging me to cast aside anything not aligned with Love. Admittedly, there were days when the temptation to retreat, remain silent, and conform was strong. It would have been much easier to fit back into the familiar mold. Yet, the call of the Spirit within me persisted, urging me to soar in ways I never had before — both spiritually and emotionally, as I was always meant to soar!

"Yet, the strength of those who wait with hope in the LORD will be renewed. They will soar on wings like eagles. They will run and won't become weary. They will walk and won't grow tired." Isaiah 40:31 GW

The journey has been challenging. There have been moments of despair, sorrow, hurt, and pain, moments I wanted to quit. But then I would find myself soaring on the winds of the Spirit, discovering the love and freedom to be myself, to love myself, and to love others, just as they are. No longer expecting them to conform to any doctrine. And it was worth it all.

Peter Lord, in his book *Turkeys and Eagles*, describes this tension.[1] Will we soar with the spiritual eagles, free to be ourselves, free of the religious chains that have held us back through self-loathing, rules keeping, denominational loyalties, dead routines, and doctrinal dogma, or trot with the religious turkeys, never flying but always looking to the skies as the eagles pass by?

Where are you on your spiritual journey? Are you at a crossroads? Are you ready to soar like an eagle, or are you still finding your own rhythm, walking at your own pace, trotting with the turkeys? Perhaps you have left the organized church altogether, disillusioned by polarization, lifeless religious rituals, and the lack of love. Maybe you have distanced yourself from church or even given up on Christ and the Christian message altogether. That is perfectly okay. You are exactly where you need to be at this moment.

Embrace it as a valuable part of your journey. I am not here to persuade you to take any specific action. My hope, however, is that you will realize that what God accomplished through Christ — His life, death, and resurrection — always included you. This gift comes without strings attached— no mandatory church membership, adherence to programs or denominations, or obligation to attend church services. In Jesus' finished work, there is an abundant life available for you to embrace right now, in this very moment. His love for you is greater than I can express and deeper than we will ever fully understand in our earthly existence.

PART TWO
LEAVING THE TRIBE

5

BEYOND DENOMINATIONS AND DOGMA

*Don't be trapped by dogma — which is living with the
results of other people's thinking.*
Steve Jobs

German inventor Johannes Gutenberg revolutionized book production with his invention of the printing press around 1440. This technological breakthrough significantly enhanced the speed and efficiency of printing. A pivotal moment in its history was during the Reformation movement in Europe. Gutenberg's press enabled the rapid production and distribution of Martin Luther's Ninety-Five Theses. Luther, a key figure in the Reformation, openly criticized the practices of the Catholic Church, and his ideas, facilitated by the printing press, spread quickly. This enabled a wider audience to access and discuss theological concepts, leading to the proliferation of Protestant beliefs.

Before the advent of the printing press, sacred texts were predominantly written in Latin, limiting their access to the general populace. The printing press changed this dynamic by facilitating the translation of religious texts, including the Bible, into vernacular languages. This shift made these texts more accessible to ordinary people, empowering them to read and interpret the Bible themselves, thereby challenging the authority of the Catholic Church.

Additionally, the printing press enabled the widespread dissemination of pamphlets, sermons, and other literature. Protestant reformers utilized this technological advancement to critique the corrupt practices and doctrines of the Catholic Church and to share their own ideas and beliefs. This expansion of printed material not only fueled public debates and influenced public opinion but also significantly contributed to the momentum of the religious reform movement.

Today, we are witnessing a new Reformation propelled by technological advancements such as the Internet, personal computers, cell phones, social media, artificial intelligence, and the emerging field of quantum computing. Like the 16th-century Reformation, this modern Reformation facilitates the exchange and debate of theological ideas through contemporary methods, thereby redefining our understanding of the church. The fact that you are reading this book is a testament to these technological advancements. Whether it is an eBook you have downloaded or a print-on-demand copy — neither of which was available just two decades ago — it represents a significant shift in how we access and engage with information.

A cell phone now provides access to virtually all the knowledge accumulated since the dawn of humanity, courtesy of the Internet. This unprecedented access allows you to go beyond the dogma traditionally taught in churches, enabling a thorough re-examination of theological concepts previously considered untouchable and unchangeable. With this wealth of information at your fingertips, you are empowered and equipped to question everything, scrutinize anything, and arrive at conclusions independently, free from the influences of your specific denominational tribe.

Social media has created a space where groups can come together and examine theological beliefs and deconstruct them to their basic foundation. Online video platforms offer vast libraries of new ideas about theology, allowing people to reconstruct healthy beliefs. Virtual meeting apps let individuals and groups meet live and have church without leaving home. As a result, the traditional idea of what constitutes a church is being fundamentally challenged.

These technological advancements have enabled me to undergo internal changes and deconstruct my theology. Without the resources provided by computers, cell phones, the Internet, and social media apps, I doubt that I would have been able to make these changes. They have been tools and catalysts in my spiritual journey of theological transformation.

Having the capability to listen to and consider concepts taught by individuals outside the usual circles of major denominational pastors, radio preachers, or Bible study teachers — who often repeated their doctrines without critical thought or critique — has significantly expanded my understanding beyond the confines of denomination and dogma. This exposure to various voices and viewpoints has been instrumental in broadening my theological perspective. However, venturing beyond denomination and dogma involves overcoming certain obstacles.

OLD WINESKINS

The adage by George Santayana, "Those who cannot remember the past are condemned to repeat it," carries profound significance, especially in the context of stubbornly holding onto ideas and practices solely out of tradition. Santayana's words urge us to embrace change and learn from history's lessons. He suggests that personal growth, societal progress, and intellectual development demand our willingness to adapt, evolve, and challenge conventional wisdom. Just as a river constantly reshapes its course to navigate obstacles, we, too, must be fluid in navigating the challenges of a rapidly changing world.

Consider the context of human advancement. Throughout history, societies that failed to adapt and clung tenaciously to archaic customs eventually faced setbacks in science, governance, or social equality. By studying the past, we gain valuable insights into the consequences of stagnant thinking, narrow-mindedness, and the refusal to question prevailing norms. Such historical understanding underscores the necessity of remaining open to new ideas and re-evaluating traditional practices for continual progress.

Yet, as we reflect on the significance of this maxim, it's crucial to exercise discernment. While progress often necessitates breaking free from the shackles of antiquated ideas, we must not discard the wisdom inherent in our traditions and heritage. The key challenge lies in discerning which aspects of the past are valuable and merit preservation and which require thoughtful re-evaluation and potential change. This insight is particularly relevant when considering spiritual maturation and the deconstruction of our theology. To avoid remaining spiritual infants, we must cultivate a greater spiritual awareness and understanding of our life in Christ, coupled with a commitment to living at a higher level of consciousness on a moment-by-moment basis. This process involves questioning the dogma and doctrine we have taken for granted. As Jesus said, new wine needs to go into new wineskins — suggesting that new understanding requires new frameworks of thought.

> *"And no one puts new wine into old wineskins; or else the new wine bursts the wineskins, the wine is spilled, and the wineskins are ruined. But new wine must be put into new wineskins."* Mark 2:22 NKJV

Jesus responded to the Pharisees' question about why His disciples were not fasting like those of John the Baptist or their own. He explained that one cannot continue living under the old covenant when the new covenant has arrived. Jesus represents the new wineskin — the new covenant — and the gospel of grace and love He brought is the new wine. Soon, humanity would live being led by the Spirit rather than by the works of the law, embracing the grace found in His finished work instead of relying on self-effort, motivated by love rather than the fear of an angry God.

The old wineskin represented my denominational loyalty, practices, and institutions, along with their doctrines and dogma. The old wine was my certainty in these belief systems, principles, values, and traditional ways of practicing "church." This certainty kept me anchored in the old ways of believing, confessing, doing, and constantly recommitting myself when things did not seem to work. My perception of grace was too narrow, and my understanding of love was too constrained. I came to realize that Jesus was much bigger and better than I had ever imagined.

Amid this significant change, I experienced a longing for the past to hold onto the non-essential elements, the old wineskins. A desire to cling to old religious comforts rather than fully letting go and receiving what had always been true but was hidden due to my closed mind and hardened heart. This tension between the comfort of what I had known and the revelation of the new truth was a challenging part of my journey.

FEAR OF BEING DECEIVED

One aspect that the Christian religion often excels at is instilling a fear of being deceived or misled by false doctrine. Yet, Jesus said the people you need to be concerned about are those in the religious establishment who proclaim Him as the Christ.

> *"And Jesus answered and said to them: 'Take heed that no one deceives you. For many will come in My name, saying, "I am the Christ," and will deceive many.'" Matthew 24:4-5 NKJV*

Note that Jesus is not simply warning against individuals claiming to be the Christ. Anyone can see through that kind of apparent deception. Instead, he cautions against the religious establishment attempting to set itself up in a position to speak for Him. He advises not to be deceived by such individuals or establishments. The nature of organized religion is to seek something of material value that can be seen, touched, or felt. It tends to be focused on the temporal to the detriment of the spiritual or the eternal unseen. A cursory review of the history of organized Christianity since the first century confirms this perspective. It suggests that deception has often been more prevalent within these religious organizations and structures than outside them.

The greatest deception focuses on a fleshly, carnal work of self-effort rather than embracing the finished work of love and grace in Christ Jesus. For centuries, the organized church has sought to "build" the Kingdom of God or accomplish something tangible for God. Even today, churches are focused on the number of attendees, the size of buildings and budgets, the acquisition of land, various programs, and carefully choreographed services of musicians and preachers designed to please the crowds. Meanwhile, the deeper spiritual needs of the congregation — the burdens, wounds, and fears they carry — remain unaddressed, leading to a façade where everything appears fine, but in reality, it is not. This is the real deception, and the very thing Jesus warned us of.

For many years, I lived within the confines of what I now see as a deception about organized Christian religion — both as a lay member and later as a pastor. I was deceived about its powerlessness, lack of spiritual life, commitment to money, property, notoriety, and unwillingness to face hard truths when a change was needed. My greatest fear was that I might be led astray if I ventured outside the comfortable boundaries of my theological tribe and its sphere of control. However, I eventually realized that the real deception was present within my own tribe and associations, just as Jesus warned. Yet, due to fear, it took me until my fifties to open my mind to the truth, to examine other viewpoints, and to be willing to change my heart.

To be clear, I am not condemning the individuals who participate in these religious organizations or the pastors who lead them. Indeed, organized churches can and do contribute many positive works, such as caring for those experiencing poverty, sickness, and other troubles and traumas. The sense of community and the opportunity to serve and support others in need and receive assistance and prayers can be deeply comforting.

However, the crux of spiritual life lies in an inner, unseen journey that manifests outwardly rather than outward works aimed at transforming you inwardly. The key distinction is between an external focus on works versus an internal emphasis on our union and oneness in Christ. This union and oneness, which we are all a part of, is spiritual and organic. It transcends control by individuals, organizations, or programs.

IS GOD AS LOVING AS I BELIEVE?

In our spiritual counseling sessions, some clients take issue with our portrayal of God as good and perfect love. They often raise questions that seem to contradict this view:

- Is He not holy and demanding of justice?
- Does He not require that justice and equity scales be consistently balanced?
- Did He not require Jesus to be sacrificed on the cross for our sins and turn away from Him in that moment because of our sins?
- Are we not appointed to live once and then face judgment, according to the apostle Paul?
- Does vengeance not belong to the Lord?

On and on go these questions, and I understand where they are coming from. I used to feel the same way and struggle with the same questions. Then, something pivotal happened that altered my perspective. During the worst moment of my life, I *experienced* the unconditional love of God — a love that has no expectations. It did not come from reading, hearing, or talking about His unconditional love. I experienced the One Who is Love. In the middle of a life-altering chronic illness that stripped away my health, job, career, finances, and future prospects, I encountered the unconditional love of a good God. A God who refused to give up on me and continued to believe in me even when I had given up on myself — the One who is Love encouraged me, held no record of my wrongs, and wanted only the best for me in every circumstance. God is love, and everything else is secondary to that perfect love. Everything.

I also learned to discern between primary truths and secondary truths. Take, for instance, a principle in science: A primary truth is that everything in the universe is composed of energy. A secondary truth is that everything is made of atoms. Is everything made of atoms? Yes, but this secondary truth is subordinate to the more fundamental truth that everything is energy at its core, whether in the form of visible matter or invisible spirit. Everything is energy.

Is God just? Yes, although most of us do not understand justice from God's perspective.[1] However, it is essential to recognize that justice is a secondary truth. This must give way to the primary truth that God is Agape Love. When we grasp the reality of His extreme love and grace, all other attributes become secondary. God's love is so immense and all-encompassing that it surpasses everything else, redefining our understanding of all His other qualities.

> *"I am convinced that nothing can ever separate us from God's love which Christ Jesus our Lord shows us. We can't be separated by death or life, by angels or rulers, by anything in the present or anything in the future, by forces or powers in the world above or in the world below, or by anything else in creation."* Romans 8:38-39 GW

> *"... I also pray that love may be the ground into which you sink*

your roots and on which you have your foundation. This way, with all of God's people you will be able to understand how wide, long, high, and deep his love is. You will know Christ's love, which goes far beyond any knowledge."
Ephesians 3:17-19 GW

God's love led me out of the legalistic, transactional, fear-based religious mindset that had characterized much of my life. I came to realize that He is not only good and loving but also infinitely kinder, more gracious, and more merciful than I, or anyone else, can even imagine.

LOVE OVERCOMES FEAR

I watched a video clip on social media that showed a woman befriending a chipmunk in her backyard. Initially, the chipmunk was skittish and would run away whenever she approached. To gain its trust, she began by sitting on her deck and tossing peanuts in the shells into the yard. Over time, the chipmunk grew bolder, venturing closer to gather the peanuts. It progressed from coming onto the deck to approaching the foot of her chair, and eventually, the chipmunk trusted her enough to take peanuts directly from her hand.

It took time for the chipmunk to overcome his fear of her. Over several months, he eventually climbed onto the arm of the chair and ate peanuts out of her hands. Eventually, he would rest on her leg, allowing her to pet him as he napped. Every time she came outside, he would come running, eager for the peanuts and the opportunity to sit in her lap. Her love and generosity had triumphed over his fear, creating a bond of trust and affection.

Love is the universal language understood by every person, animal, plant, and even the soil beneath our feet. Love overcomes fear. The Bible puts it this way:

"No fear exists where his love is. Rather, perfect love gets rid of

> *fear, because fear involves punishment. The person who lives in fear doesn't have perfect love."* I John 4:18 GW

Living in fear is the hallmark of the Christian religion. This fear manifests in various ways: fear of losing one's salvation, fear of divine punishment, fear of being deceived, fear of eternal damnation in Hell, fear of rejection by church and denominational peers, fear of displeasing God through perceived inadequacies in giving, praying, or worshiping, and fear of falling short of the ideal Christian standard. However, the true hallmark that Christians should embody is love — love for themselves and love for others.

> *"A new commandment I give to you, that you love one another; as I have loved you, that you also love one another. By this all will know that you are My disciples, if you have love for one another."* John 13:-34-35 NKJV

> *"For all the law is fulfilled in one word, even in this: 'You shall love your neighbor as yourself.'"* Galatians 5:14 NKJV

We're given one fundamental command: to love ourselves while loving our neighbor. That is it. It is all about love. Yet, in practice, fear has often been the overriding emphasis, overshadowing the principles of grace and love in Christ. As love becomes the central focus, it paves the way for deconstructing destructive theology. We become more open-minded to listening to voices outside our particular denominations and small church associations. It allows us to be more receptive to the Spirit living in us rather than being confined to years of fear-based doctrine and dogma.

We do not have to live in fear of a good and loving God, nor fear the future, the opinions of religious individuals, or falling into deception. The Spirit of Christ within us is our Teacher (John 16:13-15) and guards us against deception and stumbling. Even when we do stumble, failure is not the end; it is an integral part of our journey in learning about love. God is faithful and will walk with us, in us, and through us at every moment. Everything is as it should be; each moment is a precious gift. So, let love conquer any fear and begin the journey one step at a time, moving from a fear-based Christian religion into spiritual freedom and health in Christ.

MOVING BEYOND FEAR

A recent study found that fear of the unknown is the greatest obstacle to change.[2] Fear of what the outcome will be. People often worry about how change will affect their personal life, family, friendships, finances, and future. The more uncertain the change, the riskier it seems, leading to greater fear.

Moving beyond the fear of change starts with a change of mind and heart. If we are to break free from the chains of destructive religious systems and enjoy spiritual freedom, overcoming fear is essential. The religious fear we have been taught in church hinders us from being our authentic selves in Christ and from loving others unconditionally, just as they are.

The Greek word for "change of mind" is *metanoia*. In the Bible, it is translated as "repentance," but this translation is not what the word means. *Metanoia* encompasses the idea of seeing something from a different perspective, a shift in thinking leading to a change of heart. Over time, this changed perspective will impact one's beliefs and one's behavior. Modern translators and the church have defined *metanoia* as turning from sin, refraining from evil deeds, or believing in something non-orthodox. Nothing could be further from the truth! A change of mind and heart is an internal process, not an external one. It begins with considering something from a new perspective, leading to a change of mind, and in time, it will cause a behavioral change.

While turning from certain behaviors can result from *metanoia*, this is not the word's primary meaning. *Metanoia* involves a deep internal change of mind or heart, where we come to see God as perfect Love and truly *experience that love*. This process goes beyond merely *believing* that God can be trusted to a deep-seated *knowing* of His trustworthiness. Such realizations create a "*metanoia* moment," in which we move from fear into the boundless, unconditional love of a good God.

Love invites us to partake in the new wine from new wineskins, encouraging us to release the old wine and wineskins we have relied on for years. It empowers us to leave behind the confines of organized religion, with its denominations and dogmas, and step into the spiritual freedom found in our union in Christ.[3]

6

LOVE HERETIC

The heresy of one age becomes the orthodoxy of the next.
Helen Keller

The breakfast appointment was for 8:00 that morning. My friend was moving, and this would be the last opportunity to meet with him before he left. Greg had recently graduated from seminary and was returning to his hometown to begin a ministry position. We had gotten to know each other over several years and enjoyed discussing our seminary experiences and certain changed theological perspectives.

During the conversation, I shared with Greg how my perspective of God had shifted from Him as a judgmental, angry one who demanded holiness to a God of love, compassion, empathy, mercy, and forgiveness, even when undeserved. I had become convinced that love was who God is and that love was seen in the life of Jesus, who revealed the true nature of the Godhead. I now understood that unconditional love trumped everything.

His response was what I had expected: "That is fine, but if you teach or preach that, you will not be in the ministry long. Most Christians do not believe that, and denominations do not teach it. You will be seen as a heretic and eventually pushed out of vocational ministry." He likened my views to universalism, which believes a loving God will let everyone into Heaven in the end — a topic for another discussion. He was right. Communicating the true nature of God could lead to rejection by Christians who held traditional beliefs. How could they accept something contradicting what they had been taught since childhood? If I insisted on teaching this as biblical and spiritual truth, then I had to be prepared for the consequences — I would be seen as a "love heretic."

THE ILLUSION OF AN ANGRY GOD

In college, I attended a magic show that left me in awe of the magician's skillful sleight of hand. Each trick became progressively more challenging, yet it was all an illusion. None of it was real; it merely appeared that way. Most magic tricks divert the audience's attention while subtly executing something they are not focused on.

This is the art of illusion.

Hollywood operates in a similar fashion. What we often perceive as real backgrounds are props or studio backlots. They create the illusion of genuine homes, buildings, or roads on carefully constructed movie sets. These illusions help Hollywood save money and produce numerous films each year. Moreover, many films have actors performing in front of green screens, with backgrounds added in later. Ultimately, even the most convincing superhero's actions are just illusions.

Control within the Christian religion often relies on illusions. The belief that people will go to Hell due to God's anger over their sins drives individual attendance and church evangelistic efforts. This includes the worldwide deployment of missionaries with significant financial contributions, of which a significant percentage finds its way into the church's coffers. This belief in Hell persists despite the apparent irrationality of such eternal punishment. (A God who inflicts extreme eternal punishment for temporal failings is either psychopathic in nature or is a figment of humanity's imagination).

Furthermore, the illusion extends to the idea that God will be angry with you if you do not meet specific requirements, such as church attendance or failing to contribute to the church's activities. The emphasis on maintaining one's salvation through "righteous" behavior rather than fostering a genuine relationship with God adds to the illusion. Actions like reading the Bible, praying, giving, attending church, and witnessing are at times seen as appeasing God's anger rather than expressions of love. All of which is based on performance rather than unconditional love. If you have been unfaithful, God will use personal tragedies as a means to "get your attention," which only perpetuates this illusion.

It is all based on a theology of an angry, vengeful God whose only desire is to create fear so you will do what He wants. But it is all an illusion, like the magician's tricks and the Hollywood props. It is an attempt to control you by using the fear of an angry God to divert your attention from what is genuinely important: unconditional love that comes with no expectations.

God is love. He has no pit of fire to put you in. No vengeful desire to get back at you for your "sins." No desire to control you through fear. And He established no religious manufactured institution in this material world to put your focus on rather than on His life in your spirit. He will love you no matter what. You cannot mess everything up, ruin it, or make Him angry. He has loved you for all eternity and will love you. He wants you just as you are and requires no changes. He is good beyond explanation and more loving and compassionate than you imagine.

The church creates the illusion of an angry God to control you through fear, but as Jesus said, "You will know the truth, and the truth will set you free."

FREEDOM FROM FEAR AND CONTROL

Christian Gnosticism was a movement that emerged in the ancient world in the first and second centuries. It offered a unique approach to spirituality, focusing on *gnosis*, a Greek word that means direct experiential knowledge. Unlike traditional religious practices, Gnosticism emphasized personal revelation as the key to salvation and enlightenment. One of the significant benefits of Gnosticism was its encouragement of individual exploration and discovery. Followers of Gnosticism believed that everyone had the potential to directly connect with the Divine and gain insight into their true nature. This idea empowered individuals to develop a personal relationship with God without relying on religious authorities or rigid doctrines.[1]

Unfortunately, Gnosticism faced opposition from the rising Orthodox Christian movement. The early Christian leaders sought to establish a unified belief system and centralize their power. This led to the suppression and condemnation of Gnostic teachings, labeled heretical and dangerous. Many Gnostic texts were destroyed or lost and, as a result, limited our understanding of their unique perspectives. However, fragments of Gnostic teachings survived in the form of alternative Christian traditions and the rediscovery of ancient texts like the Nag Hammadi Library in 1945.

Today, Gnosticism continues to captivate the interest of scholars, spiritual seekers, and those who crave a more personal and experiential approach to spirituality. Its emphasis on individual revelation and a complex understanding of the universe offers an alternative perspective that resonates with individuals seeking deeper meaning and connection in their spiritual journeys.

The destruction of Gnosticism by orthodoxy narrowed the range of spiritual expression within Christianity and stifled alternative ways of approaching spirituality. It also limited our knowledge of the diverse religious and philosophical ideas that existed in the ancient world because of fear and a desire to control people, institutions, religious doctrines, and dogma.

Spirituality has always been persecuted by orthodoxy. Put another way, those who are focused on the unseen eternal things are inevitably misunderstood, persecuted, and shunned by those focused on the outer material things. Fear is a great control mechanism, an emotion that the "orthodox" Christian religion in all its various denominations has wielded for centuries to the detriment of spiritual health and inner peace.

To be sure, I am not advocating for a return to Gnostic teachings or practices. Nor do I agree with many of their doctrines. But doctrine, practices, and teachings were not at the heart of Gnosticism. Spirituality is an inner knowing and listening to spirit and true identity in Christ. This personal knowing, what Paul called "walking by the Spirit," is what orthodoxy killed. And it has been done through fear and a desire to control.

There was not a single time that Jesus used fear to control people. He never tried to coerce people to do something or make threats against them. He never threatened them with Hell or punishment if they did not get their act together or did not trust Him. Nor did He seek to control them by creating an illusion of an angry and vengeful God.

Yet, if you listen to sermons in most evangelical churches, you would think Jesus talked more about Hell than anything else (I will discuss Hell in the next chapter). Fear has been the tool that Christianity has used to control people since the second century.

Embracing the unconditional love of God, as revealed in Christ, is a transformative step toward liberation from external pressures and control. This divine love, free from expectations and conditions, empowers individuals to discover and express their authentic selves, unburdened by fear, anxiety, or the restrictive controls often imposed by religious institutions. In this context, unconditional love is not just a sentiment; it is a radical acceptance that challenges and transcends the traditional expectations and norms dictated by the church. By fully accepting this type of love, one can enter a space of true freedom, where one's identity in Christ is expressed in its purest form, unshaped by external demands or doctrines.

EMBRACING UNCONDITIONAL LOVE

The autonomic nervous system (ANS) plays a crucial role in our body's fight-or-flight response, regulating functions like digestion, heart rate, breathing, and temperature control. When we encounter danger, the ANS springs into action, triggering a series of physiological changes. Blood flow is redirected towards essential muscles, priming the body for rapid response, while less critical functions like digestion are deprioritized. The release of adrenaline and cortisol sharpens muscle reflexes and heightens alertness. Breathing becomes faster, increasing the oxygen supply to vital organs and muscles. The heart rate accelerates to support this increased circulation. Pupils dilate to allow more light into the eyes, which can be beneficial in low-light conditions. Everything operates in overdrive in this state, focusing the body, brain, and mind on the immediate threat.

Fear becomes the predominant feeling, intense and overwhelming, lasting as long as the danger is perceived. This response is automatic, beyond our conscious control, as exemplified by common experiences like a sudden scare by someone, a near-miss in traffic, or a performance review at work. Even after the immediate threat passes, the psychological impact of this intense fear can sometimes linger, affecting our mental state.

For centuries, Christians have been taught to live by their autonomic nervous system, a fight-or-flight response. This ingrained behavior acts as a "safeguard," often subconsciously, against doctrinal deviations, disagreements with established theological views, or lifestyle choices that diverge from traditional church teachings. This reaction has become second nature for some, serving to protect deeply held traditional beliefs.

The concept of embracing God as one who loves unconditionally, without expectations, challenges the "autonomic nervous system" of most Christian's theological/religious belief system. This metaphorical system, akin to the autonomic nervous system's response to physical threats, represents a psychological mechanism that activates in response to ideological threats, such as challenges to deeply ingrained religious convictions. In this context, the challenge is accepting a view of God who offers unconditional love, free from the traditional expectations or conditions often associated with religious doctrine. This internal psychological response remains in a state of constant overdrive, manifesting as stress, anxiety, and an inability to live in the moment fully.

> *"No fear exists where his love is. Rather, perfect love gets rid of fear, because fear involves punishment. The person who lives in fear doesn't have perfect love." I John 4:18 GW*

> *"I have loved you the same way the Father has loved me. So live in my love." John 15:9 -GW*

To understand First John 4:18, we must first look at John 15:9. The word for "love" in this verse is *agape*. It's a compound word in Greek from *ago*, which means to lead, and *pauo*, which means to cease or rest. Agape leads another to rest. Jesus said His love for the disciples (and us) is the same way His Father loved Him, which is agape and leads us into inner rest and peace.

How can God's love lead you into inner rest and peace? Because that is what agape does, and agape is who God is. It is His nature. Love trumps everything else. (SEE I CORINTHIANS CHAPTER 13) A shepherd oversees his flock, seeking their safety and well-being. The sheep learn to hear the shepherd's voice, follow the shepherd, and trust him.

The same is true for God. His love leads you to trust because it is unconditional and without expectations. He constantly seeks your highest good no matter what. In the same way that He loves Jesus, He loves you. You are in Christ, and He is in you. This is a mature love, a love that's based on eternal realities and not denominational dogma. He then says we are to live in His agape; we are to remain, abide, or stay in His love. Let your life be grounded in the unchanging, radical nature of God's love for you. His love will lead you to trust Him, thus enjoying inner peace and rest.

In exploring I John 4:18, we gain a deeper understanding of "perfect" love. In this context, "perfect" is translated from Greek as full-grown, mature, or complete. The Greek word for "love" here is also *agape*, signifying a mature, unconditional love that leads to inner rest and peace. This kind of love actively casts out fear. In Greek, "fear" is *phobos*, which signifies terror, alarm, or panic – states that are fundamentally opposed to the nature of agape. Fear is, in many ways, an illusion, a misbelief about oneself, God, or others that exists outside the reality of love. Fear finds no foothold when love is "perfected" or fully realized in us — in its understanding and expression. It is in understanding and embracing the full meaning of agape that fear is cast out, freeing the soul from its grip. Mature agape love does not coexist with fear; it actively dispels it. This is because mature love nurtures trust, allowing an individual to rely entirely on the one who loves them.

Embracing love is natural when your spiritual eyes are opened to the truth of who God is, who we are in Christ apart from any decisions or works on our part, and our oneness with every person we meet because of Christ.

This was true in my case. Love pushed fear out of my soul and replaced it with peace. I began to trust God as kind, forgiving, compassionate, loving, merciful, giving, and gentle. He only wanted my good and would never give up on me in this life or the next. His love is eternal, and nothing can defeat it. This is the substance of the love we are called to trust and embrace. Once embraced, this love frees us from the fear that the Christian religion has propagated since the second century. This allows us to be open to new spiritual truths and understanding to reach a higher level of consciousness for living each moment.

FEAR OF REJECTION

In many Christian communities, a subtle yet powerful mechanism of control exists, perhaps unintentionally, rooted in the fear of rejection. This fear often emerges when individuals grapple with beliefs or viewpoints that deviate from the established doctrines of their church. For instance, consider the inner conflict experienced by those who support LGBTQ+ rights or hold a pro-choice stance, even if they personally oppose abortion. Such positions can be seen as controversial or "heretical" within certain circles, leading to a palpable worry about being ostracized or marginalized by the church community. This dynamic reflects the tension between personal convictions and communal doctrines and highlights a critical challenge many faithful face: navigating the delicate balance between upholding one's beliefs and maintaining a sense of belonging within the religious community.

Codependency, characterized by a fear of rejection, a fear of abandonment, and a compulsion to control situations to avoid pain, plays a significant role in many aspects of life (refer to the chart in the book's conclusion for more details). This concept holds true in religious contexts as well. In my own experience, I have grappled with the fear that the church would cast me out, leading to alienation from its members. The anxiety of being labeled a heretic, or worse, a fallen believer, was a constant companion. This fear often drives religious individuals to conform to the expectations of pastors or elders, seeking their approval rather than following the Spirit's guidance. In my journey, I have sacrificed my beliefs to gain favor and avoid ostracism from those in religious authority. This was an attempt to control their acceptance, to remain part of the religious community, driven by the dread of the pain their rejection might cause. Instead of embracing love and grace, my actions were motivated by fear and self-effort.

Considered the most rejected individual in history, Jesus faced rejection and denial at every turn. He was rejected by members of His own family who did not believe in Him. The residents of Nazareth saw only a carpenter, not a Messiah. Jewish religious leaders perceived Him as a radical threat to their authority. The very crowds that once sought His miracles quickly turned, clamoring for His crucifixion. Even His disciples, His closest companions, abandoned Him in His hour of need. On the cross, amidst the anguish of His humanity, He experienced a profound sense of forsakenness by His Father, despite the Father's ever-present love. Subjected to mockery, spitting, and ridicule, and enduring the Romans' brutal flogging and crucifixion, He faced these trials with unparalleled resilience. "Father, forgive them, for they do not know what they are doing," He uttered, exemplifying the depth of His love. This internal reservoir of love empowered Him to extend grace and forgiveness, even amidst the deepest rejection.

When you see yourself in Christ, in union with Him, rather than separate from Him, it becomes possible to love yourself and others, even when they reject you in their confusion. Because the love that lived in His spirit lives in your spirit, as you are one with Him this moment. Love overcomes, heals, brings wholeness, encourages the heart, never stops hoping, and endures all things; love never ends.

Only love overcomes the fear of rejection because a loving God in Christ Jesus has not rejected you and never will. You are accepted, adored, valued, loved, and one in Christ. God did this long before you ever came to this planet. Religious man-made institutions and their adherents may reject us, but in union with Christ, we are accepted as much as Christ is in the Father.

Let love free you of the fear and control the church has used against you. And that love will heal you and free you to be yourself in Spirit.

ALL IS WELL

I have come to embrace the label of "love heretic" with pride, seeing it as a badge of honor. Our purpose here is to learn the art of love — loving ourselves, loving others, and accepting God's love. This journey of learning and growing in love, I believe, is the very essence of our existence on Earth. In loving ourselves and others, we are loving God.

Embracing this path meant facing rejection from some in the institutional church and certain family members and friends. The cost of this spiritual freedom has been high, but the rewards — the inner peace and rest I have gained — are invaluable. The acceptance of an artificial religious system pales in comparison to the authentic peace I now experience.

Echoing the words of Julian of Norwich, "All shall be well, and all shall be well, and all manner of things shall be well." I have found this to be a profound truth. No matter what transpires, in union with Him, all is indeed well, and all will be well.

7

RECONSIDERING CORE THEOLOGICAL BELIEFS: PART ONE

Progress is impossible without change, and those who cannot change their minds cannot change anything.
George Bernard Shaw

In an intriguing study known as The Five Monkeys Experiment, researchers observed the behavior of monkeys within a managed setting. They hung a bunch of bananas from the ceiling, but whenever a monkey attempted to grab them, all group members were doused with cold water. This collective punishment created an uncomfortable experience for all of them.

As a result of this repeated punishment, the monkeys quickly learned to avoid reaching for the bananas to prevent the unpleasant consequences. Over time, they associated getting the bananas with adverse outcomes and stopped trying altogether.

After some time, the researchers introduced a new monkey to the group, replacing one of the original monkeys who had undergone the cold-water punishment. Unaware of the history of punishments, this new monkey naturally tried to reach for the bananas. However, it was swiftly discouraged by its peers, who had internalized the avoidance behavior.

This process repeated itself as more new monkeys were introduced. They, too, adhered to the group's established norm, refraining from reaching for the bananas, even though they had not directly experienced the punishment themselves. This perpetuation of learned behavior among the monkeys highlights the powerful influence of group norms and social learning.

Just like these monkeys, some Christians hold on to beliefs because of their church and denomination's beliefs or what the pastor taught them. Anyone who tries to climb higher on the theological ladder to a new and different perspective is pulled down and beaten up emotionally and mentally.

Fear of God's anger, the church's reaction, and the uncertainty of change pull people down and hold them captive to the religious organization's belief system. This prevents freedom of independent thought and the spiritual growth that goes with it.

Navigating the journey of spiritual deconstruction required me to first confront and then overcome the deep-seated fears associated with questioning my long-held beliefs. This process was not merely about shedding old notions; I needed to reconsider what the Bible taught, who Jesus really was, why I believed what I believed, and the source of fears that had shadowed me for years.

It involved touching the untouchables — such as the inerrancy of scripture, Hell, an angry and vengeful God, salvation, and my part in the kingdom, to name a few. This path is not for the faint-hearted, but it is not impossible. Throughout this process, one is never truly alone; the Holy Spirit acts as an ever-present guide, offering direction and comfort regardless of where you are on the journey. This spiritual guidance extends to everyone, including those who do not identify as believers.

This chapter covers some more prickly theological topics that once hindered my spiritual progression and how I worked through them. Certainly not in exhaustive detail, but I hope to share my experiences to assist you on your own path. The intention is not to prescribe beliefs or dictate stances on these matters; instead, I wish to leave the interpretation and decision-making to your discretion, leaving that between you and God.

INERRANCY IS UNNECESSARY

"I believe the Bible's the Word of God, and it is inerrant and infallible from Genesis to the maps!" If I heard that once, I heard it hundreds of times from more preachers than I can count. Their interpretation of the Bible was predominantly literal, rarely from a deeper spiritual one. My first question was always: "What does that mean?" Considering the Bible encompasses sixty-six books penned by various authors over a span of sixteen hundred years, each with its unique purpose and audience, the statement felt overly simplistic. Yet, this was the belief system I adopted, influenced by the teachings of my church and denomination.

This leads us to unravel three critical questions:

1. The definition of the "Word of God."

2. The meaning of "inerrant."

3. The understanding of "infallible."

From an Old Testament viewpoint, the Torah, prophets, psalms, and other Jewish scriptures are the word of God. In these texts, authors often claim to convey messages directly received from God. To the Jews of Jesus' day, these writings were all considered to be the word of God. However, it is essential to recognize that these scriptures — referred to as the Old Testament in Christian tradition — originate from the foundational covenant of circumcision established with Abraham, the laws given through Moses, the establishment of the Kingdom of Israel under David, and the prophesied promises of a coming Messiah for Israel.

From a Christian perspective, the old covenant should be perceived as obsolete; it was only a shadow of the good things to come. It was replaced by the new covenant in the person of Jesus Christ, the Messiah, in whom God reconciled all things and people to Himself — past, present, and future — without exceptions or exclusions.

Unlike the old covenant, which is rooted in texts and laws, the new covenant is not based on the written word but is embodied in a Man, Jesus Christ, who has risen from the dead. Our faith is to be anchored in the completed work of Christ for all time, independent of human actions, including traditional rituals like the unnecessary "sinner's prayer." This perspective emphasizes a direct and personal relationship with God through Jesus, transcending the written word.

The concepts of inerrancy and infallibility are not necessary because the new covenant is grounded not in a document but in the personhood and the fulfilled promise of God in Christ. Jesus is the Logos of God. He alone is the Word of God, not the Christian or Jewish scriptures. Our relationship is with Him, not a book. The advent of the new covenant marked the end of the law, the old covenant of circumcision, and the reliance on self-effort and performance. It signified a departure from a rigid set of rules, principles to live by, or commands to obey.

Under this new covenant, grace becomes the operative principle, signifying that salvation is an unearned gift rather than the result of human endeavor. This grace implies that everything necessary has already been accomplished; there are no prerequisites or conditions to fulfill. You are complete just as you are. Enjoy it!

As this took hold in my heart, I began to look at the scriptures differently, seeing them from a spiritual perspective rather than as a collection of principles to adhere to or theological doctrines to defend as church dogma had taught. Instead of a literal, inerrant viewpoint, I began to see the scriptures through spiritual eyes. I began to engage with the scriptures through a spiritual lens, appreciating the Bible as a servant of Christ and a source of comfort and support in our relationship.

By approaching the Bible from a spiritual perspective, the stories, parables, and teachings opened to me in new and incredible ways. The Bible became a support, among many other sources, in my relationship with God in Christ. I no longer needed to defend and guard its integrity or insist on a uniform belief in its interpretation.

The necessity for the Bible to be inerrant — that is, incapable of error — diminished because the work of God in Christ Jesus is sufficient. Similarly, the requirement for it to be infallible — incapable of mistakes — became redundant, as Jesus Himself is the Word of God. The completeness of the covenant in Jesus means that the potential for errors or inaccuracies within the scriptures (inherent in all human-authored works) does not detract from the truth and power of God's message. The focus shifts from the written word's literal perfection to the perfect work of redemption and relationship completed in Christ.

Having no more need for unnecessary debates on the inerrancy and infallibility of scripture brought me inner peace and rest. It allowed me to focus on what was important: my union in Christ.

HELL'S ILLUSION AND CONTROL

When I was twelve, our church participated in an evangelistic event at a high school football stadium. These events typically took place every evening from Sunday to Wednesday one week in the summer. The evangelist was always well-known as a Hellfire and brimstone guy. Toward the end of the week, he would preach a message on Hell, sin, and the judgment to come. He would ominously claim that someone would die within 24 hours of his sermon, using fear to coerce attendees into repentance to avoid being the next victim. His desire was to control and manipulate his audiences to walk the aisle "for repentance" from fear they might be the ones God killed that very night.

This tactic not only manipulated people into conversions but enhanced his success rate, which increased the likelihood of securing future invitations to preach. This was the type of behavior I grew accustomed to within the evangelical church.

My mother, deeply influenced by her denomination and prone to fear, fell for this scare tactic — taking the bait hook, line, and sinker. On the way home, she took extra precautions: insisting on seat belts, opting for safer roads, and enforcing immediate bedtime upon arrival, coupled with thorough security checks that doors were firmly locked and staying awake all night just in case someone tried to break in. All because a manipulative evangelist tried to pad his numbers with a portrayal of a vindictive God, ready to send anyone to Hell who didn't walk the aisle after hearing his sermon.

For centuries, the illusion of Hell has been manipulated to instill fear and control over people. The threat of eternal damnation for not believing in Jesus or losing salvation due to misconduct has been a common scare tactic. The ambiguous standards of what constitutes a "true christian life" further exacerbate this fear, leaving many to wonder whether they were ever saved at all, unknowingly destined for Hell. This notion is enough to cause sleepless nights. In my role as a spiritual counselor, I witness the emotional and mental toll this form of spiritual abuse takes on individuals, with nearly every client wrestling with these deep-seated fears.

I, too, have delivered sermons on Hell and damnation as a pastor, believing I was helping my congregation. However, in reality, I was unknowingly abusing the people I wanted to help.

After stepping away from vocational ministry, I began diving into the scriptural basis for the concept of Hell, a doctrine seemingly embraced by many Christians and society at large. This fascination with a place of punishment for the "bad" people, a realm of justice and suffering for wrongdoers, led me to doubt its existence. Is Hell really in the Bible? Is it reflective of the person of Jesus Christ and the finished work God completed for all people in Him?

RECONSIDERING CORE THEOLOGICAL BELIEFS: PART ONE   73

While this book is not about the doctrine of Hell, my investigation of it in the scriptures and reflection on the nature of Jesus Christ and God's redemptive work led me to conclude that Hell is not what we were taught after all. The conventional teachings on Hell do not align with the underlying textual realities in the Bible, nor does it align with a God of unconditional love. Knowing this has liberated me to live in the reality that God loves me unconditionally and would never hurt me. And you can live in this freedom too.

The word "hell" does not appear in the surviving Greek manuscripts of the New Testament scriptures as it is not a Greek word but instead originates from the old Germanic language deeply rooted in Nordic mythology. Its first recorded usage dates back to 725 A.D. Its first appearance in a Christian context is found in Dante's "Inferno" around 1317. It was not until the 16th century that English translators of the Bible started to interpret the Greek words *Sheol, Hades, Gehenna,* and *Tartarus* as "Hell," even though none of these words meant a place of eternal torment. Their translation choices were driven by an attempt to consolidate various concepts into a singular notion of a punitive realm for nonbelievers or fallen angels despite the distinct original meanings of each term.

Sheol is a Hebrew word meaning unseen or the grave, referring to a burial pit where a body is laid to rest and thus becomes unseen. In the context of the Old Testament, the concept of Hell as it is understood today was unfamiliar to the Jewish people, as such an idea does not exist in the Torah or other Jewish scriptures. Regrettably, translations of the Bible have often rendered *Sheol* as Hell, a gross misinterpretation aimed at reinforcing certain theological doctrines.

Hades, a word derived from Greek mythology, referred to a realm where all souls were believed to go upon death, serving as a sort of holding place rather than a place of torment. *Hades* was used metaphorically, typically within the parables, to illustrate a point (though Jesus did not speak Greek but Aramaic). The gospel writers used *Hades,* a Greek word, as the best explanation of what Jesus was saying. It was not to develop a theological doctrine of damnation. The translation of *Hades* as "Hell" in Christian texts reflects the development of Christian mythology over thousands of years and was used by translators eager to support their version of an angry and wrathful God.

Gehenna, on the other hand, was a physical location — a garbage dump outside of Jerusalem where trash and the bodies of the deceased, particularly the destitute and executed criminals, were thrown away and incinerated. This site's continual fires made it a potent symbol for the Pharisees, who used *Gehenna* to depict the fate awaiting those who defied the law of Moses or were unbelieving Gentiles. Jesus employed the concept of *Gehenna* in his parables to highlight grace and the new covenant established in Him rather than lay the groundwork for a doctrine centered on punishment. Using imagery traditionally associated with legalism, He repurposed it to underscore messages of grace and love, effectively challenging the prevailing interpretations with a transformative perspective.

Finally, *Tartarus* originates from Greek mythology, where the ancients believed that the souls of foreign soldiers who died in battle against Greece and other "wicked" souls were confined and tormented in the Earth's center. In the New Testament, the word *Tartarus* is only used once, in II Peter, referring to fallen angels who were held there until the end of the ages. It is never used pertaining to human punishment in the scriptures and should not have been translated as "hell."

Based on these facts, I concluded that Hell was not only an illusion but a tool used by institutional Christianity over thousands of years to control the masses, a strategy that has proven effective and, regrettably, continues to be so.[1]

Shedding this false doctrine was like a weight lifted from my soul, and I began to enjoy the unconditional love of a good God who has no expectations and loves and accepts me just as I am. This realization, however, does not negate the fact that we can create our own version of hell here on Earth. The history of human conflict, the mistreatment of the vulnerable, and the escalating acts of violence are stark manifestations of the torment we inflict upon ourselves and others when love is absent from actions and priorities.

"SINNERS" IN THE HANDS OF AN ANGRY GOD

Jonathan Edwards, an 18th-century American pastor and evangelist, delivered a sermon he had written titled "Sinners in the Hands of an Angry God" in Northampton, Massachusetts. It was later published in July of 1741. This sermon, which played a crucial role in sparking the First Great Awakening in America, emphasized the wrath of God towards sinners and His readiness to cast the "wicked" into Hell at any moment.

Edwards depicted God as a Judge who condemns and punishes, creating Hell as a place for those who fail to trust and love Jesus. The sermon utilized fear of eternal suffering, the prospect of irrevocable rejection, and being tormented by "Satan" as tools of control and manipulation, urging listeners to convert and "trust" in Jesus. Tragically, the sermon's grim message led to profound hopelessness among several of Edwards's parishioners, with instances of suicide reported, including one individual related to Edwards himself.

From its inception, the sermon ignited controversy, yet it remains celebrated by some within the evangelical community as one of the greatest sermons ever given in Christianity. Edwards' portrayal of a wrathful God, eager to punish the "wicked," persists in American pulpits today, albeit with a moderated tone and more compassionate approach. Nonetheless, the tenets remain intact: a portrayal of a relationship with God as transactional, whereby safety from His wrath and rejection hinges on compliance with His demands. The message is that you are not safe from Father God's anger, punishment, and ultimate rejection unless you do what He wants you to do. This interpretation of the gospel is void of unlimited grace, unconditional love, unending mercy, or tender compassion. It suggests that divine acceptance is contingent upon human action rather than bestowed freely and lovingly by God.

Edwards' theology, particularly his views of God's love and the nature of salvation, including his stance on slavery, reflects a profound deficiency in spiritual understanding despite many still seeing it as the gold standard of theology. His acceptance of slavery underscores the necessity for continuous growth in our understanding of God, ourselves, and others in union with Christ.

The damaging impact of doctrines promoting a literal Hell and an angry, punitive God has been profoundly negative, influencing numerous lives across and beyond the Christian community for almost three hundred years. These teachings have led to widespread theological confusion and a deep-seated emotional disconnect from God. Depicting God as relentless, harsh, and eager to punish mirrors the dynamics of an abusive relationship characterized by impossible standards, continual highlighting of failures, and fear-driven compliance.

When people make decisions under duress or intimidation, the relationship is tarnished and damaged. It casts doubt on the sincerity of actions — are they motivated by genuine desire or fear? The integrity of the relationship is compromised because of fear.

Consider one example of an argument against an angry God. What if I told my wife when I asked her to marry me, "Cyndi, I love you, and I want you to be my wife. I will give you a few days to think it over, but if you do not say 'yes' and love me, I will torture you for the rest of your life." What woman in her right mind would answer yes? But this is how Christianity misrepresents a loving God who only wants to show us His love in Christ Jesus.

I Corinthians 13:5 makes it clear that love keeps no list of wrongs. God, who is love (I John 4:8), keeps no list of wrongs against you, nor does He desire to punish you. You are His creation in Christ, a masterpiece of His design (Ephesians 2:10; Genesis 1:26). When my heart shifted away from a God of anger, punishment, threats, and control to one of love, compassion, mercy, and giving, my soul began to enjoy inner peace. I was freed from feelings of being controlled, manipulated, or threatened. I discovered a relationship with God where he respects my choices and is with me through all of the consequences of my decisions without ever forsaking me or judging me. Even in the absence of my love or obedience, God's love remains unwavering, always ready to forgive and extend His hand in kindness. He is never offended, never disheartened by my actions, and His commitment to me is eternal. This is the Divine Source of life who exists.

The god of Jonathan Edwards? I do not know him because he does not exist. Edward's god only exists in the imagination of those Christians who have made an angry god the foundation of their faith and beliefs.

A FINAL WORD

In this chapter, we have looked at the question of inerrancy of the scriptures, whether there is a literal Hell, and the nature of God as love versus Edwards's angry, punishing god. These are only examples of my own process of deconstruction and determining what I actually believe. As I wrote earlier, it is not a comprehensive study of each theological tenant or the process of deconstruction. I wrote this as a guide in your own journey of coming out of past destructive dogmas that have hindered your inner peace and spiritual growth.

In the next chapter, we will unpack three additional theological tenants:

- What is salvation?
- Is God angry with people?
- Does God's Kingdom need our efforts?

8

RECONSIDERING CORE THEOLOGICAL BELIEFS: PART TWO

Man cannot discover new oceans unless he has the courage to lose sight of the shore.
Andre Gide

When scientists believe something is settled science, it can be a bit unnerving to find out that it is not. This was true for astronomers who were studying the images from the James Webb Space Telescope. In reviewing the images, they discovered that there were galaxies younger than 700 to 500 million years old that are as big as our Milky Way galaxy. The Milky Way Galaxy is considered to be 3.5 billion years old, so these newly discovered galaxies that are so much younger should not be that big.

According to most theories of cosmology, galaxies are formed from small clouds of stars and dust that gradually increase in size. In the early universe, the story goes, matter came together slowly. But that does not account for the massive size of the newly identified objects. [1]

Even though scientists believed they had settled the matter regarding how large a younger galaxy could be, they were forced to reconsider their beliefs and change course to adapt to new discoveries.

When someone challenges what you believe to be settled theologically, it, too, can be a bit unnerving. We have been taught to believe certain theological truths without question. Yet, Jesus never told His disciples not to question and continually discover the truth. Rather, He encouraged them to see things in a new light, from a new perspective, and be willing to change their minds.

As we go through this exercise of questioning, examining, and discovery, lay aside your fear of change and embrace the unending possibilities. Be willing to cast out into spiritual depths and leave the safety of the known theological shoreline. You may find settled theological matters that are actually unsettled, and in the process, discover a new perspective that opens you to new spiritual growth and enlightenment.

SALVATION IS NOT FROM YOUR SINS

Salvation and sin are complex and loaded topics that this book cannot fully explore, nor is it my intent to do so. Since the birth of the church at Pentecost, the study of salvation has been a focal point of theologians and scholars. This specialized study is known as soteriology. Similarly, the interpretation of sin has evolved over thousands of years. Is sin the things we do that fall short of God's standard? And if so, what standard? The old covenant is gone (it was only a shadow, to begin with), and the new covenant in Christ Jesus the Messiah is the fulfillment of all that was promised. There are no standards, just Christ's finished work of grace and our life in Him.

This section aims to briefly deconstruct what we have been taught about salvation and sin and how that can enhance your faith journey. To achieve this, we will also explore the evangelical consensus on the theory of atonement and its significance. My goal is to present these ideas clearly and simply.

The Greek word for salvation, *soteria*, encompasses meanings such as deliverance, preservation, safety, and salvation itself. The preference for translating *soteria* as salvation rather than its other meanings has been influenced by prevalent theological interpretations, particularly within Protestant and evangelical circles. This choice is largely shaped by the widespread acceptance of the Penal Substitutionary Atonement Theory (PSAT) among these groups.

There are at least eight different theories regarding Christ's atonement, a fact that may surprise many given the predominant adherence to PSAT across evangelical, some Protestant, and even Catholic traditions. PSAT asserts that Jesus' death as the Son of God served as the substitute for the punishment deserved for our sins. According to this theory, God is holy and can have nothing to do with sin and, by extension, with sinners — all of humanity whom He created. His justice, therefore, requires payment for sin, either from the sinner or a proxy.

Jesus, through His virgin birth, sinless life, and sacrificial death, fulfilled this role, absorbing God's wrath and justice on our behalf. His resurrection signifies the acceptance of this sacrificial payment, thereby reconciling humanity with God and ushering in the new covenant in Christ. This covenant opens the door to direct communication with God. Your part is to believe and trust Christ, repent of your sins, and live in this new life. By embracing this belief, God's Spirit comes to dwell in you. However, some hold that this indwelling of the Spirit happens later — once a person has grown more mature in their faith.

In a nutshell, the belief is that because God is holy and is angry about sin, He must demand punishment and payment for it. Yet, out of His love, He sent His Son to bear His wrath, allowing Jesus' sacrifice to cover our sins so God can offer forgiveness instead of eternal punishment in Hell. This forgiveness, however, hinges on a sincere faith in Christ and true repentance. It is transactional.

Therefore, the term "salvation" is preferred by evangelical translators over words like "deliverance," "preservation," or "safety" because it fits the theological narrative of PSAT. This perspective, however, presents God as wrathful and retributive, diverging from the compassionate nature of the Godhead as represented in the person of Christ Jesus.

If it is not love, mercy, kindness, peace, joy, forgiveness, empathy, and gentleness, it is not Jesus. Therefore, it is not God. Love trumps everything with God.

Nor does PSAT take into consideration the union of all things in Christ. The reality of a finished work in Him includes all people!

PSAT fundamentally relies on fear, which is contrary to the nature of agape love (I John 4:18). Fear finds its origin in the creation story of the tree of the knowledge of good and evil versus the tree of life, which metaphorically represents Christ Himself. He is love, and there is no fear in love. None.

The term "salvation" implies an escape from punishment or God's wrath and misses the reality of what we have been freed from. Deliverance is a more accurate description. But what exactly have we been delivered from?

While sin is part of what we are delivered from, more crucially, we are delivered from the law — specifically, the obligation to fulfill its demands through our own efforts and performance, which inevitably leads to failure.

> "Sin is what gives death its sting, and the Law is the power behind sin." 1 Corinthians 15:56 CEV

This comes back to our life, death, and resurrection in Christ. When He lived, we lived; when He died, we died; and when He rose, we rose with Him. His life is our life.

Paul explains in Romans 7:1-4 that our union with Christ's death freed us from our marriage to the law, much like the death of a spouse releases us from the bonds of marriage. This concept goes back to the story about Adam and Eve's choice to live under the law (self-effort) by eating from the tree of the knowledge of good and evil instead of choosing union with the divine life in the Spirit (tree of life). When Christ rose, we rose with Him, united with Him through grace and love, released from the impossible demands of the law.

Now, we live by the Spirit, free from the constraints that once bound us, embodying the life of Christ's Spirit in us, which is one with us. The law's power is broken because we are married to another; we are spiritually married to Christ. This message of love, grace, and liberation is the heart of the gospel, extending to every person across all time.

The translation of the Greek word for "sin," *hamartia*, has been problematic because it does not have anything to do with evil behavior, breaking God's laws, immorality, or vices of any kind. *Hamartia* combines *ha*, meaning no or not, with *martia*, derived from the root word *mores*, which means form, portion, or lot — implying a deviation from one's true form or identity. The word finds its origin in the Greek tragedies. It was descriptive of the protagonist in the Greek tragedy and described the fatal error the protagonist would make due to a lack of information or a misunderstanding of something.[2] This fatal error is not due to any moral wrong or evil intent but to the wrong information or misunderstanding that the protagonist would rely on for a decision, resulting in the error itself.

Later, *hamartia* was used as an archery term to signify missing the mark of the target. The archer's failure to hit the mark could be due to various factors like incorrect assessment of distance, wind conditions, or the archer's technique. None of these reasons for missing the target relates to the conventional moral implications associated with our understanding of the term "sin."[3]

When we fail to grasp our identity in Christ — with Him dwelling in us and us in Him — we mirror the tragic hero by mistakenly believing that following rules, adhering to standards, or obeying laws through our own efforts can make us acceptable and good. The moment we succumb to trying to achieve something beyond the finished work of Christ, we stray from the truth of our existence in Him. *Essentially, we strive to accomplish what God has already completed through Christ.*

Our true inheritance is inner rest and peace, found in trusting and listening to the Spirit at every moment. We stray from this path when we fail to recognize God as a loving and kind Father with whom we and others are intimately connected in oneness, sharing in His life and love together. This oversight exemplifies the essence of sin, aptly describing it as "missing the mark."

Christ came to deliver us from a false sense of self, the constraints of legalism, and, ultimately, the destructive cycle of self-effort that traps us in a never-ending cycle of self-judgment. That then extends to judging and condemning those around us. Our misconstrued concept of sin keeps us yoked to the metaphorical tree of the knowledge of good and evil, constantly striving yet never reaching the imposed "standard." Christ's death was not to atone for "bad" behavior or to correct an inherent flaw within us. Rather, it served to liberate us from these constraints, thereby illustrating agape love and revealing our true identity in Him. To see Him is to see ourselves. To know Him is to know ourselves. To behold Him as in a mirror so we might understand ourselves fully.

You were (in God's eyes) included in His birth, life, and death and raised with Him as He is to live in your true identity, which is your spirit. Spirit is the essence of who you are and always has been.[4] Realizing this begins the liberation from the fear-filled punitive doctrines of PSAT and the notion of an angry God into the reality of the love and union you have in Christ at this moment. This understanding frees us from fear, allowing us to live with inner peace and rest in our souls.

CHRIST IS NOT ANTI-ANYBODY

During a session, a counselee I had been working with for several months asked if God hated her because she was gay. I had wondered whether she felt this way, but I wanted her to bring it up when she was ready to discuss it.

I reassured her: "Jesus is not anti-anyone. Your feelings of self-loathing, influenced by others' words or actions, or perhaps a preacher's condemnation, do not reflect God's view. He loves you as you are — without conditions, without demands for change." Her smile and look of relief signaled, perhaps for the first time, a deep sense of being accepted, loved, and valued as she was.

I am learning to love people where they are, as they are, and for who they are at this moment without seeking to change them, imposing demands, or offering unsolicited advice. Our sole responsibility is to love others unconditionally. This is the way of Christ Jesus.

The belief that it has been our job to change others has no place in true Christian practice. Instead, our role is to love each person God brings into our lives. Part of my journey involved deconstructing harmful beliefs ingrained by an evangelical Christianity that condemned LGBTQ+ individuals, those who are pro-choice, and anyone who challenged their narrow interpretation of the Bible and man-made doctrines.

Nothing could be further from the life of God in Jesus and the truth of who all are in Him. Embracing the truth of God's love in Jesus and recognizing the divine image in all people has been both healing and transformative, enhancing my ability to love genuinely and see everyone as inherently worthy of God's love, as God's creation, united in Christ Jesus. (See Ephesians 2:10)

I have had enough of the hate and misogyny preached from the pulpit, all stemming from fear — fear of differences, fear of losing control, fear of seeming inferior. I reject this fear. God is not anti-anybody. His love is boundless and inclusive, and it flows through you and me, enabling us to love and connect with others, regardless of how they see themselves. *That is the way of Christ Jesus.*

GOD'S KINGDOM DOES NOT NEED OUR EFFORTS

Christianity has a long history of sending missionaries worldwide to spread the gospel. Evangelism has been a central focus, at least in the denomination I grew up with. The message was clear: We must labor to bring in the harvest.

> " ... 'The harvest is plentiful, but the workers are few. Therefore, ask the Lord of the harvest to send out workers into his harvest-ready fields.'" Matthew 9:37-38 NET

"Work" is a gross misrepresentation of the meaning of this verse. However, it has been used to provide people with a goal, something to strive toward, and a purpose both individually and as a community of believers. It also served as a catalyst for pastors, denominational leaders, and others to initiate evangelistic programs, recruit "workers" in these efforts, and motivate financial contributions so that those believed to be "dying and going to Hell" could hear the gospel. This approach proved to be a highly effective business plan.

In verse 38 of Matthew 9, Jesus is not instructing His disciples to physically toil to bring in the kingdom. He encouraged them to pray, focus on the spiritual rather than the material, and ask the Lord, who is the God or Source of the harvest, to send workers into the harvest.

What was the harvest? People. People whose hearts long to hear and experience the message of grace, compassion, love, and mercy. The message is that God in Christ has done everything necessary, and following a "standard," striving through self-effort is not required. Instead, come to Jesus, lay down *all* of your efforts, and find rest. Let the Shepherd of your soul care for your inner life.

Spiritual people show this message of completeness, love, and acceptance by the simplicity of their actions in everyday life. There is no kingdom to build, no missionary endeavor to embark on, no denomination or church to establish — just love by the Spirit in you. It is beautifully simple yet often-rejected by Christians who desire tangible tasks and goals. They overlook the deep, unseen, and eternal reality in the Spirit.

When I gave up on "building the kingdom," I joined God in loving people daily. He brought people from all over the world to me. There was no longer a need to actively seek baptisms, membership commitments, financial contributions, witnessing, or other church-related activities aimed at "building the kingdom."

There is nothing to build; there is simply a kingdom in Christ to enjoy in His playground of love and grace. Everyone is included, whether they are actively engaged, unaware of the privilege, or even oblivious to the existence of the kingdom. Everyone exists in the realm of grace and love. Will you embrace the radical love and grace of our loving Father, have some fun, and play in His playground called life in the Spirit?

A FINAL WORD

These are just a few of the theological sacred cows I had to deconstruct in my spiritual journey. There are many others.

Deconstruction can be like attempting to escape from a constantly shaken snow globe. I do not expect you to arrive at all the same conclusions I have. Maybe you will, or maybe you will not, and that is perfectly fine. What is important is allowing the Holy Spirit to lead you into spiritual freedom, away from the safety of the denominational theological shoreline, and into the depths of His love.

It is entirely acceptable to work through your questions and reach certain conclusions and yet still have more questions about the same concepts or doctrines. I am still in the process of deconstructing myself;

it is an ongoing journey with no final destination. However, I am taking one step at a time, gradually healing and recovering from years of religious abuse that kept me confined within a theological box.

Let the light shine in, maintain an open mind, let go of fear and anxiety, and trust yourself in the hands of the Divine, who loves you more than you can imagine. But Scott, *"What if I am deceived or believe something I should not believe?"* Trust yourself and Christ to guide you where you need to be. Sometimes, we need to get off the familiar path to explore and broaden our horizons, but we are always on the way to the summit.

Enjoy every moment of the journey and remember that it is not your responsibility to maintain theological balance; that role belongs to the Holy Spirit. Let Him do His job while you relish in the exploration, expansion, and growth of your spiritual journey.

9

LEAVING THE TRIBE OF MY FATHER AND MOTHER

My dear terrified graduates, you are about to enter the most uncertain and thrilling period of your lives.
Lin-Manuel Miranda

During my high school graduation, on the cusp of adulthood, not yet eighteen, I was acutely aware that life as I knew it would never be the same. The familiarity of walking through the school halls, the routine of baseball practices, and the comfort of classroom discussions in English Literature and Social Studies were about to become memories. The realization was bittersweet. I would only return as a visitor. My friends and I prepared to part ways, each embarking on our unique journeys. It was a difficult but necessary transition. My gaze turned toward college, a horizon brimming with promise and challenge.

Four years later, I graduated from Oklahoma State University's School of Business. Those four years opened my eyes in humility to how little I knew. The bittersweet realization dawned on me once more: My days of attending classes here, of being engulfed in the vibrant campus life

— the thrilling football games, the late-night study sessions that stretched into the wee hours, and the juggling act of fitting in intramural sports between business law quizzes — had come to an end. I would never walk these grounds again, except as a visitor. My connection to this place was forever changed. As my friends and I ventured forth, seeking our destinies, I was again reminded of the inevitability and necessity of transition and change.

Eleven years post-college, I stood at another commencement, this time at Southwestern Baptist Theological Seminary, holding my Master of Divinity. Those intensive three years were a humbling journey that revealed how much more there was to learn. The daunting tasks that had become my routine, such as crafting a 25-page exposition on Karl Barth's *Christology*, backed by a dozen sources, or navigating twelve hours of Greek, would no longer be part of my daily life. Once more, I realized that my connection to this place would, from here on, be as an alumnus. My peers, too, would scatter, each pursuing their calling. This transition, like those before it, was challenging yet essential.

Growth and learning require change and an open mind. I would not be the person I am today without the willingness to learn, grow, and change. Embracing new understanding often requires letting go of former ideas. Moving forward requires leaving behind old wineskins to enjoy the new wine of fresh insights and experiences.

The same is true of our spiritual journey. In our spiritual development, the time will come to graduate and move on to a new adventure of understanding and growth with new ideas and challenges. If you are reading this book, the time has likely come.

Transitioning from a strictly religious identity to a more open, spiritually inclusive perspective is often challenging, particularly when one has deep ties to a specific denominational or religious community. This shift represents a significant crossroads — one that is inevitable for those on a spiritual journey. Embracing this path leads to greater spiritual freedom, inner peace, and a sense of liberation and rest.

REALIZING I COULD NOT STAY

One Sunday, as I listened to the pastor's message, one thing became clear: If I were going to grow spiritually, I could not stay where I was; *something needed to change*. My theology and spiritual awareness had grown, and the messages no longer resonated with me as they once had. It was like trying to find depth in the innocent babble of a toddler — charming and necessary for their stage of development but not for fulfilling my needs.

Compelled by this realization, I retreated to the foyer mid-sermon, turning to my phone in search of a church that might be a better fit for where I was spiritually. I found a possibility, and my wife and I visited the following week. We attended the new church until the COVID-19 pandemic hit, when we, like many churches, transitioned to online services. Once the COVID restrictions were lifted two years later, it was again time to move on due to my theological and spiritual growth curve.

Leaving was a difficult decision. We had made some friends there and really liked the pastor. However, it was clear that our theology and inner spiritual life were again outgrowing where we were. Additionally, my involvement with Abiding in Agape, which focuses on counseling those coming out of toxic religion toward God's unconditional love, demanded more of my attention. I also felt led to write books to reach even more people.

Currently, I don't belong to any particular church community. Instead, I enjoy fellowship with many believers outside of an institutional church format and the counselees seeking guidance in our spiritual counseling practice.

This does not imply that leaving your church is a prerequisite for questioning your beliefs or advancing spiritually. While staying is less common, it is entirely possible. However, it is crucial to be prepared for the challenges that accompany staying where you are. I will address remaining in your church in the final section of this chapter.

LEAVING AND THE SENSE OF LOSS

There is a concept called entrainment[1] illustrated in a YouTube video where five metronomes are set to 176 bpm (beats per minute) and mounted on a foam core board. This board is then balanced on several empty cans and is free to move from side to side, enabling the metronomes to eventually synchronize with each other due to their interconnected movements. Once the cans are removed, the metronomes are no longer physically coupled, and some fall out of step.[2] This is similar to trying to stay in a church with which you no longer share theological or philosophical alignment. Just as the metronomes fall out of step without a shared base, maintaining congruence with a community becomes challenging when foundational beliefs diverge.

Experiencing the departure from something or someone you love, whether it is through death or divorce, inevitably brings about a sense of loss and a period of mourning. The healing process can take months, years, or even decades, depending on the individual and the loss. It takes time to let go and move on. This gradual journey through grief and acceptance also applies when distancing oneself from a familiar church community. The bonds formed within such a setting are deep and multifaceted: It may be where we deepened our faith, married our spouse, or witnessed our children forging their own spiritual and social connections. The pastor of this community might have played a pivotal role in your family's milestones, further entwining your life with the fabric of the church.

As you navigate the upheaval of re-evaluating your theological and spiritual beliefs, the weight of leaving behind a community that houses many personal milestones and relationships can feel particularly burdensome.

Leaving the churches that we were deeply integrated with brought about a tangible sense of loss. The close friendships we once had changed as we found ourselves outside the circles we once belonged to. The deconstruction of theological beliefs can create a wedge separating us from those who continue to adhere to the doctrines we once shared because we may no longer believe the way they do.

It had not dawned on me how crucial it was in our churches to maintain a uniformity of theological beliefs, with little or no room for disagreement. It seemed as though there was an unspoken rule to leave critical thinking at the door. Their sense of security did not stem from the finished work of God in Christ but from the assurance that their tight-knit circle shared identical beliefs and never rocked the boat. This realization only magnified the sense of loss we felt upon our departure, highlighting the depth of the communal and ideological divide.

But mourning, grief, and sorrow do not last forever; they eventually give way, allowing you to progress in life and in the work the Spirit started in your heart. While a sense of loss may linger, along with a yearning at times for the familiar comforts of the past, the desire for spiritual growth is greater. The choice stands between remaining in a spiritual kindergarten, comfortable and secure in your beliefs, or graduating to higher levels of spiritual understanding, where beliefs and perspectives are continuously examined and expanded. I chose the latter, and the amazing benefits that followed justified the decision.

FRIENDS, FAMILY, AND OTHER DISASTERS

While vacationing in St. Petersburg, Florida, surrounded by white sandy beaches, I started writing my first book, *Alignment of Authentic Love: Living Your Highest Life*, and was excited about working with the editor I had chosen. A thousand miles from home, I hoped for peace, soaking up the sun and enjoying the seagulls as I worked on my book. Instead, I experienced firsthand the outcomes of my theological and spiritual awakening.

On the first day of our vacation, I began receiving emails from a close family member expressing concern for my spiritual "well-being" after I had shared some of what God had been teaching me recently. The emails questioned my departure from what they called "fundamentals of the faith" and included video links of evangelical Christian fundamentalists. As a seminary graduate, former pastor, and someone who reads the Bible in Hebrew and Greek, I found these emails condescending, annoying, and unnecessary. However, they also provided an opportunity to articulate my beliefs further.

Throughout my vacation, this family member persisted in debating my beliefs, sending lengthy emails with additional video links. In response, I would offer a brief, pleasant reply, thanking him for his concern and suggesting some great books to better understand my perspective, proposing that once he had read them, we could have a more informed conversation. He did not take me up on the offer.

Midweek, I received an unexpected email from my editor informing me that she was no longer interested in editing my book due to what she termed "theological heresy." Having only worked through the introduction and first chapter, she expressed that she was not impressed with my theological stance and could not, in good conscience, contribute to a work she believed would lead so many people "astray." The search for an editor had been exhaustive, involving months of vetting and discussions to ensure potential candidates were comfortable with content that might challenge traditional theological views. She initially seemed receptive and agreed to work with me. However, that quickly changed, leaving me with a project in limbo and several sections only partially edited. Finding a replacement proved challenging, as I worried other editors might also balk at my emphasis on God's love instead of religious dogma.

Over the next few years, persecution continued in various forms. Friends publicly called me out on social media for emphasizing God's unconditional love, as if I were a heretic needing to be exposed. I had also receive phone calls from people offering to "counsel" me about my theological stance and questioning my departure from what they considered "the faith given to the saints."

I clarified to them that I had not abandoned my faith and did not require their help. It did not matter how much I explained why I had changed and the focus on God's love; they would not listen. In their view, I was wrong, and they were right because their church believed in the orthodox position. Some even felt duty-bound to "save" me from Hell and God's punishment, even though they could not explain why a message of pure, unconditional love would warrant such punishment.

This situation underscored the reality that many Christians are unaware of why they hold certain beliefs, having never examined and challenged them for themselves. Some resist considering alternative perspectives, fearing the impact on themselves, their families, and their social connections within their church communities. I understand now why revolutionaries who challenge the prevailing norms are often burned at the stake.

This is the path of those who go from Christian religion to spiritual freedom in Christ. I knew it would cost me something, but not to the degree it has. It is much easier to go along with the crowd, accept their dogma and doctrine, and not make a fuss. Such conformity could have secured me a position of power and influence within the church's hierarchical system, along with the praise of my fellow brethren and the comfort of belonging. But I couldn't do that. That path was empty, hollow, and unfulfilling. It prioritized outward appearances while neglecting the internal life of my soul and spirit. To me, it was a dead and rotting system, and I was all too aware of its stench.

WALKING THE LONELY WAY

In the days after Pentecost and the revealing of the Holy Spirit within people, early believers were known as followers of the Way, a term referenced in Acts 9:2. Later, in Acts 19:9, this same phrase is also applied to the local church in Ephesus. Then, as Paul stood before Felix to defend himself against the accusations of Jewish religious leaders, he acknowledged that this group, referred to by critics as a sect, followed the way of Jesus. (SEE ACTS 24:14)

Jesus was someone they hated and eventually crucified. He challenged their mindsets and religious ideas. He ate with sinners, feasting and celebrating with them, actions that deviated sharply from the strict adherence to the law of Moses expected of good, devout Jews. He rejected the heavy religious rituals that burdened the people with an exhaustive list of rules. Instead, He exposed the hypocrisy of the religious leaders and attracted large crowds who came to be healed and listen to Him teach.

> *"Come to me, all you who are weary and burdened, and I will give you rest. Take my yoke on you and learn from me, because I am gentle and humble in heart, and you will find rest for your souls. For my yoke is easy to bear, and my load is not hard to carry."* Matthew 11:28-30 NET

Jesus was all about love, leading people to inner peace of soul. Love would nourish them and release them from the burdens of the endless cycle of attempting — and failing — to adhere to rigid laws and regulations. He offered them freedom from legalism, accusation, and fear, offering them radical grace and love that required nothing of self-effort.

The term "Christians" was first used to describe the followers of Jesus years later in Antioch, eventually becoming the predominant label and overshadowing the original designation, "followers of the Way." This shift in terminology is regrettable, as "followers of the Way" is more accurate. The Way is unconditional love devoid of expectations, condemnation, or obligations. It is marked by accepting people just as they are, without the need for rules, doctrinal affirmation, or denominational allegiances to define or constrain one's faith. Paul described it this way:

> *"For the whole law can be summed up in a single command-*

ment, namely, 'You must love your neighbor as yourself.'"
Galatians 5:14 NET

Jesus exemplified divine love for humanity, demonstrating through His life and teachings that love is paramount to God. His ultimate act of love was His selfless sacrifice, dying under false accusations while extending forgiveness to those responsible for His death. (SEE LUKE 23:34)

However, the institutionalized version of Christianity often emphasizes a narrative of an angry God of retribution and condemnation. This perspective portrays a God who punishes those deemed unholy or evil, condemning them to eternal damnation for failing to uphold His standards of holiness. The concept of a God who loves unconditionally, without any prerequisites or expectations, is frequently dismissed or labeled as heretical.

Living the Way of Jesus can often be a lonely path embraced by only a minority. Despite the loneliness this path may entail, I have discovered a profound sense of inner peace and rest — a feeling *I NEVER* experienced during my time as an evangelical pastor. The depth and tranquility of my inner life is so much more excellent!

The question boils down to this: Are you enjoying inner rest and peace promised to you in Christ? Is life simpler, relaxed, and less stressful, free from internal stress? And have you entered the rest that the writer of Hebrews emphasizes? (SEE HEBREWS 4:3-11)

WHAT IF YOU DECIDE TO STAY?

To be clear, I am not suggesting that everyone must leave church due to changes in their theological and spiritual perspectives. Some people remain within their church, navigating the journey of their theological deconstruction while maintaining and enjoying the connections they have built over time. Staying or leaving is a personal decision; the key is to choose what feels right for you and to be prepared for the implications of that choice.

For me, leaving was the better choice. I have never experienced a greater sense of freedom, calmness, and joy than I do now, away from the organized institutional church. It simply was the best path for me. It would feel like reverting to elementary school while pursuing a PhD — too much growth and progress has been made to return. And I am at peace with that.

Should you decide to remain within your church and denomination, here are a few things to consider:

- Be aware that the majority within your church may not embark on the same theological and spiritual journey you have. It is important to find peace with this fact. If you cannot, it might be wiser to leave.
- Your spiritual progress might proceed more slowly within the organized church than outside it. Remember the principle of entrainment, in which pace and direction are influenced by those around you.
- Develop relationships outside your church with people who are also on a journey toward spiritual freedom. Social media platforms can be valuable for connecting with like-minded people. There are many social media groups that offer a safe place to work through theological and spiritual questions. Building relationships that provide encouragement and support will be helpful.

Regardless of your choice, be prepared for the moments of loneliness that will occur when it feels like no one else understands. This is an opportunity to listen to your spirit, come to know yourself better, and embrace your union in Christ.

PART THREE
HOPE AND HEALING

10

FREEDOM TO LOVE YOURSELF

Love yourself first and everything else falls into line. You really have to love yourself to get anything done in this world.
Lucille Ball

From her earliest memories, Taylor was deeply rooted in the evangelical Christian tradition. Her parents were very committed to their church, denomination, a literal view of scripture, and the Bible as the inerrant word of God. She committed her life to Christ at a young age and was baptized. In junior high and high school, she would attend youth camp and continuously rededicate her life to Christ during one of the services, hoping to live a more Godly life.

By the time she graduated from high school, she was thoroughly indoctrinated into and fully committed to the Christian worldview. She wholeheartedly believed in the gospel message and the teachings about God's judgment and the dire consequences of Hell for those who did not repent and believe in Christ.

In college, Taylor's world expanded significantly. She began to make new friends, some of whom were not believers. Contrary to her expectations, she found these new friends to be kind and fun, introducing her to new ideas about the world and religion she had not explored before. Simultaneously, some of her coursework presented perspectives and theories that caused her to question and re-evaluate the religious doctrines ingrained in her since childhood.

This began a long journey of theological deconstruction and freedom from the idea that something was wrong with her or that God was to be feared rather than enjoyed.

Before graduating from college, Taylor began to question her church's teachings about various groups, especially LGBTQ+ people, and those not professing Jesus as their Savior. She began doubting the existence of Hell, the devil, and the inerrancy of the Bible. Taylor also explored theories about Christ's atonement that did not align with the idea that He died for our sins to satisfy God. She grew weary of fearing relationships with those who did not believe as she did or those who were gay or lesbian. Above all, Taylor struggled to feel good about herself and began questioning her innate worth and value.

Concerned, her parents invited their pastor to talk with her, but the conversation left Taylor feeling minimized, disrespected, and threatened because of her doubts and questions about church doctrines and pastoral authority. Her uncle, a minister, called her to help "set her straight" and get her back on the right path. However, his approach, marked by disrespect for her beliefs, only worsened the situation. Taylor felt so alienated that she became uncomfortable attending family gatherings.

At thirty, recently married and supported by her husband's encouragement to be true to herself, Taylor publicly shared her evolved theological viewpoints on social media. This move exposed her to further persecution from church leaders, her family, and friends. Despite the criticism, she chose to be honest and transparent rather than hide in the shadows.

Taylor and her husband decided to change churches and find a community that would welcome their beliefs and feelings without judgment. However, after several years of visiting churches, talking to pastors, and praying about what they should do, they chose to step away from organized religion altogether. This decision marked the beginning of Taylor's healing from deep-seated feelings of inadequacy and the fear ingrained by religious teachings.

Her relationship with her family remains tense due to her beliefs, and many former church friends from her previous circles have distanced themselves, no longer responding to her texts or unfriending her on social media. All this came from her decision to think for herself, re-evaluate her beliefs, and let go of those she could no longer endorse. For her, God's love took precedence over rigid religious doctrines, biblical literalism, or any denomination's rules.

RELIGIOUS ABUSE

Marlene Winell, a San Francisco-based therapist with a background in fundamentalist Christianity, authored *Leaving the Fold*, a book detailing her journey away from her strict Christian denomination. The book explores her experiences of religious abuse, her decision to leave church, and her path toward healing and recovery. Here is an excerpt from her book:

> "In conservative Christianity, you are told you are unacceptable. You are judged with regard to your relationship to God. Thus, you can only be loved positionally, not essentially. And, contrary to any assumed ideal of Christian love, you cannot love others for their essence either. This is the horrible cost of the doctrine of original sin. Recovering from this unloving assumption is perhaps the core task when you leave the fold. It is also a discovery of great joy — to permit unconditional love for yourself and others."[1]

This highlights two central harmful beliefs: First, that people are born flawed because of "original sin," and second, that they are always in danger, either from being punished by God or being led astray by others. These ideas cause deep self-hatred and constant fear. People worry that they are never good enough; even if they follow the faith, they might not meet all the standards or could be tricked by others into making mistakes. There is also the fear of the Devil's tricks. The underlying message conveyed is one of perpetual fear, emphasizing a constant state of vigilance against deception.

This contradicts the understanding we are to have that we were created by God, His very idea, which implies a sense of responsibility on His part. Yet, this dualistic message warns of eternal punishment if we do not freely choose to love, honor, and obey Him. Additionally, while we are commanded to forgive our enemies, God holds the power to withhold forgiveness indefinitely. This feels like "do as I say, not as I do," reminding us of flawed human parents rather than a God of unconditional love.

Religious abuse stems from these two damaging ideas: the belief that something is inherently wrong with you and that there is always something to fear. This chapter will examine the freedom you can experience in loving yourself, rooted in the understanding that nothing is inherently wrong with you. We will also look at the journey of moving from paralyzing fear to embracing God's unconditional love, which comes without any expectations. Experiencing this freedom becomes real when you're liberated from the dehumanizing doctrines and controlling influences of religion.

LOVING THE PERSON IN THE MIRROR

Christian religion instilled in me, from an early age, a deep-seated self-loathing. This message was hammered into my psyche every Sunday and Wednesday night: "Something is wrong with you." The doctrine of original sin, with its notion that I had inherited Adam's fallen nature and, thus, was inherently unacceptable to God, became ingrained in my identity from my earliest memories. Over time, this belief led me to despise myself and others because if something was wrong with me, there must also be something wrong with them.

My parents struggled with their own issues of self-esteem from their upbringing. It was difficult for them to give me something they had not fully received: self-love and acceptance. So consequently, I internalized their low self-esteem, which played out in every relationship in my life, but none greater than my relationship with myself and God. I could never love myself because God could not accept me as I was, as He created me. There was a pervasive belief that something about me was inherently flawed and needed to be eradicated.

Looking in the mirror was torture. Though a daily necessity for tasks like brushing my teeth or combing my hair, it was the most challenging part of my day, as the reflection staring back at me was someone I truly despised. Over time, this self-loathing took a toll on my nervous system, leading to a life of constant anxiety, stress, and fear.

When I first became ill with the neurological condition, it felt as though God wanted to convince me He was perfect love and assure me that He had always loved me unconditionally, regardless of my actions or circumstances. That is the essence of radical grace. Grace knows no boundaries, rules, or prerequisites; it is freely given without any strings attached. As the revelation of God's unconditional love penetrated my fearful heart, I slowly began to grasp this reality. I realized that I would be loved no matter my choices or words. Even if I turned away from God, He would continue to passionately love me throughout eternity without any conditions or demands — just pure love.

This revelation opened the door to loving myself. After years of struggling, I could finally look at that guy staring back at me in the mirror and love him. Not because of my actions, adherence to rules, or attempts to be perfect but simply because I was created to be loved and inherently deserving of love. No amount of failure, self-loathing, or past mistakes could change God's mind or His unwavering love toward me. He loved me despite my imperfections, mistakes, and sins, which I had spent years trying to overcome.

Loving myself after years of being bombarded with the message that something was inherently wrong with me was nothing short of a miracle. Every day, I had to muster the courage to look in the mirror and say, "I love you, Scott. You are wonderful. God loves you unconditionally, just as you are." While that may sound corny to some people, it was, in fact, the hardest thing I have ever had to do. The depth of hurt and pain from years of religious abuse had left me feeling imprisoned in a theological dungeon of death. But as I embraced the truth of God's unconditional love, I began to break free from those chains and step into the life I was created to live — one where I could be authentically myself without seeking the approval of religious figures.

Over time, the constant anxiety, stress, and fear that had plagued me disappeared, and I began to enjoy being myself. I could finally look at the guy in the mirror and love him. Most importantly, I tended to the emotional wounds inflicted by years of religious trauma, nurturing them with love and care rather than allowing them to fester in fear and anxiety. Where there was once anxiety, I now found peace, and in place of stress, I discovered inner calmness. I became willing to accept whatever life threw my way, knowing that regardless of the outcome, I was held in the embrace of divine love.

LOVABLE, ACCEPTED, AND VALUED

Every child deserves to grow up knowing three fundamental truths: that they are loved just as they are, accepted just as they are, and possess inherent value and worth. These foundational concepts are necessary for a healthy self-identity and for establishing and maintaining meaningful relationships.

However, the Christian religion has often strayed from these principles. Over time, the focus shifted toward a legalistic approach where one's actions define their identity.[2] Within just a century of the birth of the church, church fathers began emphasizing adherence to rules rather than embracing grace.

Being deemed a "good Christian" became contingent on attending Mass, partaking in sacraments, working for the church, moral behavior, and upholding orthodox theological beliefs. Yet, none of this had anything to do with love, grace, and a completed work in Christ. Moreover, they failed to address the core needs of acceptance, value, and the reality of God's unconditional love for each individual.

You are inherently worthy of love simply because God says you are. From the very beginning, you were made in His image and likeness — an eternal spirit living and experiencing life in a physical body and with a soul, one with the Divine. Your acceptance is not contingent upon any work you do or fail to do. Your identity was established by God long before you arrived on this small planet in a vast universe. While your actions do have consequences, they serve as opportunities for learning, growth, and change.

Acceptance is based on the reality of union with the divine life. This union grants acceptance for who you are now without any conditions or prerequisites. As a beloved child of God, you are embraced as an integral part of the divine family, with equal standing and acceptance alongside every other member. This understanding frees you to love and accept yourself, irrespective of past failures, mistakes, or actions. Your value is immeasurable and beyond dispute.

Jesus came and suffered, not to save you from your sins[3] but as an example of sacrificial love to demonstrate the incomparable value placed upon you.

> *"Greater love has no one than this, than to lay down one's life for his friends."* John 15:13 NKJV

When I began to embrace and love myself for who I truly was, much of the inner tension that consumed me began to fade. Looking at myself in the mirror, I could extend love to that guy, flaws and all. My worth was no longer contingent upon adhering to a set of religious or societal standards; instead, it was rooted in the unchanging acceptance of the Divine.

Conveying this mindset to those still entrenched in the religious matrix can be challenging, as it is often misconstrued as self-centeredness or ego. Even those outside religious circles may struggle with this concept, yet adopting healthy self-love and acceptance is essential to leading a balanced and productive life. Without it, loving others becomes an errand in futility.

Leaving behind the confines of the Christian religion — Churchianity — has enabled me to love myself, which, in turn, has empowered me to love other people more authentically. I have come to understand that everyone, regardless of their beliefs, actions, or perceived identity, is worthy of love and acceptance.

CELEBRATING YOUR HUMANITY

Alexander Pope's timeless words, "To err is human, to forgive is Divine," encapsulate a deep truth about the human experience. Loving oneself is an ongoing process that only you can undertake. Celebrating your humanity (flaws and all) is essential in this process.

Being human means we are prone to errors and mistakes. As Jesus said, we are like sheep who wander off into all kinds of problems. Yet, He loves you as His own, no matter who you are or what you have done. Knowing this, you can forgive, let yourself off the hook, and embrace your humanity. Yes, we have all messed up, but that is the beauty of this life. Mistakes are how we learn; there is no other way. If you wish to learn and grow, you need to fail. Failure is part of the journey on earth. It is a necessity.

The focus of the institutional church has been pristine behavior, what they would call "holiness."

Instead of embracing humanity's frailty and failures, many within the church are conditioned to conceal them, don a mask, and pretend everything is fine. However, failure is a necessity for personal growth and learning. Through failure we learn to love and accept ourselves just as we are.

Without experiencing failures and setbacks, you would not be the person you are today — someone reading this book, questioning your beliefs, and seeking truth.

Embrace your uniqueness and celebrate this journey free from the years of false teaching that instilled feelings of unworthiness and sinfulness before God. Love who you are as you are at this moment because when you love yourself, you are loving God, who created you in His image and likeness.

11

FREEDOM TO LOVE EVERYONE

One can only learn to love by loving.
Iris Murdoch

Various attitudes and beliefs have divided people since the beginning of time. Walls of every kind have been built between individuals, groups, and nations. From racial, ethnic, and cultural divides to socioeconomic and social status, as well as religious separations, our differences sometimes create obstacles to unity and peace.

Of all the divided groups, there may be none as divided as those within the Christian religion. Being exclusive in the name of holiness may be Christianity's biggest sin. Our own statements of faith often separate people with various "church" versus "unbeliever" debates. The tendency to harbor suspicion and fear toward relationships outside of our belief system often leads to an inflated sense of superiority among those adhering to religious doctrines. This mindset is characterized by "I am saved and bound for Heaven, and you are lost and headed to Hell," making it impossible to relax and simply love others without criticism, judgment, or condemnation. The very things

Jesus taught His followers to avoid are often practiced by most Christians today.

THE INS AND OUTS

The Greek word translated by Bible translators as "church" is *ekklesia*. This term is a compound word from *ek*, which means "from, from out of," and *kaleo*, which means "to call." Therefore, a fitting definition of *ekklesia* would be "called out from."

Your mother calling out to you to come home for dinner when it is ready provides a good illustration of the meaning of this word. She calls you *out of* playtime with others *to come* and join the family meal. In ancient Greece, *ekklesia* originally referred to an assembly convened at the public place of council for the purpose of deliberating, usually of city elders and others chosen to oversee the city's affairs.

Bible translators have rendered this word as "church," which is not correct. *Ekklesia* should be translated simply as "the assembly." Alternatively, you could think of it as an assembly of those who have heard and responded to the call.

Who is issuing the call? It is the internal call of the Spirit, extending love and inclusion in Christ's finished work for all people. Just as your mother calls you and your sibling to dinner, that call is for both of you. Even if you are the only one who heard her, you would inform your sibling that it is time to go home because "Mom is calling us." This analogy beautifully illustrates the essence of *ekklesia*.

The *ekklesia* is merely an assembly of those who have heard and responded. Christianity has distorted this concept, creating a division between themselves and those outside their group. They perceive others as outsiders, rejecting Christ and engaging in evil, while seeing themselves as insiders, accepting Christ and abstaining from evil. This interpretation doesn't align with the true meaning of *ekklesia*.

The call is universal and extends to everyone. Some individuals, like the sibling in the example, may be unaware of the internal call of the Spirit, while others may have heard it but chosen to ignore it, while still others have heard and responded. Regardless of one's response, the call encompasses all and includes them as part of the family.

The call is not contingent upon one's decision or attempts at repentance to avoid punishment in Hell. Rather, it simply beckons individuals to turn inward to Spirit rather than outward to material things, including Christian organizations, methods, and plans.

The true essence of the call is to go inward to that which is eternal, significant, and real: your union and oneness in the Divine life. It invites you to recognize and embrace the reality that you are loved, cared for, and accepted. This was the intent of Christ's life and His ministry, though it is not what we often see in Christianity today.

Ekklesia is not a club or religious institution crafted by man to divide people. It is simply a manifestation of the call and the results of that call for those who have heard and responded in Spirit. When we see and grasp this truth, loving ourselves and others becomes easier, less fearful, and more fulfilling. You can be yourself with anyone, regardless of their sexual orientation, color, culture, political views, or religious background.

Ekklesia should be something that unites humanity in the reality of God's love, as seen in Christ's life. It is first and foremost rooted in the Divine Spirit because the new covenant transcends outward rituals and practices. Instead, it is founded on an inner reality of the Spirit accessible for all people, for all time.

GOD LOVES EVERYONE WITHOUT CONDITIONS

In my previous book, *Alignment of Authentic Love: Living Your Highest Life*, I addressed the topic of loving others. I use this excerpt from that book to help set up the rest of this chapter.

Regardless of whether a person ever enjoys the benefits of being in Christ, they are included in His finished work and the love of God, just as you are. God loves them completely and unconditionally, just as He loves you. His love plays no favorites. Christianity tends to "exclude" people based on what they believe about the Bible, Jesus, salvation, the gifts, and other theological golden calves...How can we say we love our brothers and sisters in Christ when we cannot be in the same room with them because of their beliefs? The modern-day organized church has emphasized purity in what you believe to the exclusion of love, compassion, mercy, forgiveness, grace, and long-suffering. We cannot abide by anyone who does not see things the way we do. So, we split into thousands of separate groups and boast of our statement of beliefs. God is not impressed with our beliefs if we do not prioritize love, kindness, and compassion. Jesus illustrated love in His parables. He showed love in how He treated people through forgiveness, healing their illnesses, touching the untouchable, hanging out with sinners, and protecting an adulterous woman. This is the person Christians say they follow, but the evidence does not match the talk. Another example is how we tend to view people as "in or out," whether they are believers or not. Have they said "the prayer" or not? Are they "conservative" enough to belong in our church? If so, they are in and going to Heaven; if not, they are out and going to Hell. These people are under His "blessing," while these others are under His "judgment" (as though we are still living under the old covenant and Christ never came to earth). The mindset is one of exclusion, of us vs. them. This is not the viewpoint Jesus had or the early church. Who gave us the right to judge anyone? Ever? Our only mission is to love people, regardless of what they have done or are doing. None of this is "love your neighbor as yourself." That statement is the key. You cannot love your neighbor while hating who you are as God's creation, made in His image and likeness. It is impossible. If I do not love myself, the true self that I am in Christ, it becomes impossible to love others for who they are in Christ. We will always see them as excluded, outside God's love, and unworthy of our love.

Jesus' life and words make it unequivocally clear that He loves people just as they are, unconditionally and without any prerequisites. When I began to grasp the depths of this reality, it was like being freed from a long imprisonment in a dark cell into the liberating light. I also realized that if I did not learn to love myself as someone created in the image and likeness of God, I could never extend genuine love to others free from ulterior motives or desire to change them.

But how can Christians love themselves when they are constantly preoccupied with the fear of making mistakes, moral failings, or sin? This belief in an inherited flaw leaves no room for loving others just as they are.

God's love, however, knows no bounds or conditions. He loves everyone unconditionally long after their body is dead, decayed, and gone. He loves them amid their greatest problems, sins, mistakes, and greatest failures. His love extends to each of us regardless of whether we reciprocate it or not. This is the central truth at the heart of the gospel: the spiritual reality that love is not for sale, cannot be earned, and can never be burdened until it is exhausted or eventually gives up. Love never fails. (SEE I CORINTHIANS 13)

FREEDOM FROM JUDGMENT AND CONDEMNATION

A friend of mine was watching a gay pride parade during Pride Month. He witnessed Christians carrying signs that were defamatory towards those who marched in the parade, hurling insults and condemning them to Hell. My friend walked over to one of the protestors and asked why she was being rude and insulting to the participants of the parade. He explained that he was a Christian and former pastor and reminded her of Jesus' command to love others. Indignantly, she defended her actions, saying, "These people are going to Hell for their abominations and wickedness towards God. God is angry with the wicked and will judge them for their sins. You, having been a pastor, should know better."

At that moment, a transgender person walked up and said, "There is no use arguing with her; she will never change her mind." Instead of aligning with hatred, my friend put his arm around the transgender person and said to the woman, "If I have a choice of identifying with you and your hatred or with him in love, I will do the latter every day." This decision only further angered the protester, who proceeded to lash out at my friend, condemning him to Hell for his compassionate attitude toward "sin."

For many who grew up in evangelical, Catholic, or Protestant denominations, condemnation and judgment were ingrained as part of their religious upbringing. To be clear, there are churches that practice kind and loving acts toward those outside the church structure. Yet for most, fear-based sermons and self-loathing were common, leading to a natural inclination of criticism and barriers between themselves and those outside the church.

The confusion stems from a misunderstanding of the new covenant in Christ and the end of the covenant of laws and rules. The old covenant is no longer valid or applicable to anyone today at all. It has been done away with.

> *"Not that we are adequate in ourselves to consider anything as if it were coming from ourselves, but our adequacy is from God, who made us adequate to be servants of a new covenant not based on the letter but on the Spirit, for the letter kills, but the Spirit gives life." II Corinthians 3:5-6 NET*

Now, liberated by the Spirit of Christ dwelling within us, we are empowered to love others unconditionally, free from judgment, condemnation, or criticism. Our actions do not define us; our identity can only be found in the finished work of God in Christ's Spirit — this is the new covenant that includes all people.

> *"For the love of Christ controls us, since we have concluded*

> this, that Christ died for all; therefore, all have died. And he died for all so that those who live should no longer live for themselves but for him who died for them and was raised. So then from now on we acknowledge no one from an outward human point of view. Even though we have known Christ from such a human point of view, now we do not know him in that way any longer. So then, if anyone is in Christ, he is a new creation; what is old has passed away — look, what is new has come!" II Corinthians 5:14-17 NKJV

Just as Christ died for all, in His finished work, all died with Him. And just as He rose, all rose with Him. You are now connected to everyone everywhere in Christ, free to no longer judge anyone from an outward point of view. We can love others from the reality of their union and oneness with God in Christ. All humanity is a new creation in Christ — together in union, free to show love, compassion, understanding, tolerance, and mercy. This is the way Christ showed us to live.

EVERYONE SPEAKS THE LANGUAGE OF LOVE

Many people who come to my spiritual counseling practice have gone through difficult traumas, have been hurt by those close to them, or have been disappointed by life and God. They hold grievances against those who have hurt them and also against themselves for their poor choices and actions in the past. They are worried about the future and whether they can ever fix all the problems they are experiencing.

But I have discovered that they all know the language of love. They know when they have experienced love. Most have little experience with being loved and more experience with being hurt or let down. But when someone faithfully meets with them, showing up every week, that is usually more than they have ever received from others. When someone listens to them with a desire to understand and empathize, it is usually more than they have ever experienced. And when someone shares the truth about how God loves them and tells them they are lovable and worthy of love, that is more than many have ever known about who God is and who they are.

The apostle Paul put it very well when he wrote about the true nature of love in I Corinthians 13.

> *"Love is patient. Love is kind. Love isn't jealous. It doesn't sing its own praises. It isn't arrogant. It isn't rude. It doesn't think about itself. It isn't irritable. It doesn't keep track of wrongs. It isn't happy when injustice is done, but it is happy with the truth. Love never stops being patient, never stops believing, never stops hoping, never gives up. Love never comes to an end. ..." I Corinthians 13:4-8 GW*

Everyone speaks the language of love. They do not always know how to describe it or explain it, but they know when they experience it. Those who follow Christ were given one job: to love everyone.

> *"Love each other. This is what I'm commanding you to do."*
> *John 15:17 GW*

> *"For all the law is fulfilled in one word,* even *in this: 'You shall love your neighbor as yourself.'" Galatians 5:14 NKJV*

The Greek word for love in the scripture passages mentioned above is *agapao*, which signifies a love that is free from condemnation, judgment, expectation, or limits. We are empowered to love every person just as they are, regardless of their religious beliefs, perspectives, or affiliations. We can extend love to the LGBTQA+ community, to those who hold differing views on abortion, to individuals outside our political affiliation, and to those who may differ from us in appearance, thought, or speech with joy and respect. In the new covenant, we are free to love every person as one with us in the love and Spirit of Christ, as this love resides within us and empowers us to do so. We can have friendships with anyone, no matter who they are, without succumbing to fear or prejudice.

However, genuinely loving others is impossible if you do not first love and accept yourself. Self-loathing breeds disdain for others because viewing oneself as unworthy of God's love and grace leads to perceiving others in the same light. To loathe yourself is inevitably to loathe others. Conversely, when you love yourself, it frees you to speak the universal language of love in each moment and with every person, regardless of circumstances or surroundings. Ultimately, love transcends all boundaries and is understood by everyone, regardless of their background or identity.

LOVING PEOPLE WAS ALWAYS THE POINT

The point of Jesus' life and ministry was to love people. His purpose was not merely to fulfill prophecy and establish moral codes, nor to issue warnings about punishment in the afterlife. Instead, Jesus came to demonstrate what genuine love looks like. He personified compassion by feeding the hungry, healing the sick, and extending kindness to the marginalized. He was friends with those whose lives were considered wicked and immoral. Jesus challenged hypocrisy and injustice while loving and enjoying life with people from all walks of life, emphasizing acceptance and forgiveness.

Jesus' actions exemplified His unwavering commitment to love and compassion. He protected a woman caught in adultery and displayed respect and empathy to the woman at the well, regardless of her past. Jesus accepted rejection as the pathway to loving others and as an inevitable part of loving people. He persisted in His ministry without seeking personal recognition or wealth, nor did He write a book. Unlike many leaders, He did not establish formal institutions nor ask anyone to form a specific religion bearing His name. Loving people unconditionally was always the point, not establishing a religion.

Sadly, over the last two thousand years, many who profess to follow Christ have veered off course, losing sight of love. Instead of prioritizing love, Christianity has become entangled in regulations dictating behavior, belief, and religious social circles. The focus has shifted to material possessions, including land, buildings, and power structures, none of which were emphasized by Jesus or the apostles. In the process, the inner spiritual life, esteemed by God, has been overshadowed by external concerns.

The primary mandate of Christianity is simple: Love people! We have fallen short of this mandate because loving others is one of the most difficult tasks one can do. Why is it so challenging? Because love inevitably entails suffering. Jesus's ministry of love culminated with His crucifixion at the hands of the very people He loved. It is far easier to instill fear and propagate judgment than to extend unconditional love beyond the confines of one's religious tribe.

The world is not moved by Sunday morning rituals, trendy music, or fitting into religious molds. What resonates is love — the universal language that drew large crowds to Jesus, compelling Him to minister in open fields.

Despite any religious directives, you have the freedom to love yourself and extend that love to others. You, like Jesus, can create a scandal by loving the seemingly unlovable and giving priority to love just as He did, *even if it means defying traditional norms and doctrines.* Love transcends all else; it is the essence of existence.

Regardless of your background, ethnicity, sexual identity, gender, or religious affiliation, the Spirit of Divine Love resides within you, empowering you to embody Love in every interaction. Make love your focal point and witness the transforming impact it has on both you and the world around you.

12

FROM CHURCHIANITY TO SPIRITUAL FREEDOM

We are not human beings having a spiritual experience. We are spiritual beings having a human experience.
Pierre Teilhard de Chardin

Imagine you and I decide to visit a church today, whether with denominational ties or entirely independent. Our experiences would likely start with the vibrant atmosphere of a worship service, where a worship team leads the congregation in contemporary songs, the lyrics projected for all to see. This communal singing creates a powerful sense of unity and participation. Following that, we would be invited to contribute to the church's mission through an offering, an act symbolizing both generosity and commitment.

Then, the core of our visit would unfold with a sermon. Lasting 30 to 45 minutes, this message is crafted to motivate, challenging us to abandon certain sins, adopt new beliefs, and implement actionable steps toward personal or familial transformation. The speaker would likely teach from the perspective of the doctrine of Penal Substitutionary Atonement. This theological doctrine suggests that humanity, flawed at its core, necessitates divine intervention. According to this view, Jesus' life and death were required to appease God's wrath against human sin, presenting a narrative in which acceptance of this sacrifice is essential for redemption from our inherent defectiveness.

In some churches, a call to action might culminate in an altar call, where there is an invitation to come forward to make a decision for Christ and accept Him into their "hearts," rededicate their life to Christ, or ask for prayer.

Membership classes offer a next step for those interested in joining the church, requiring agreement with the church's doctrinal statements. Beyond this point, many opportunities unfold to engage with the church's life and ministries, encouraging daily Bible reading and praying, faithful attendance to church and giving, evangelism, and adherence to a lifestyle congruent with the church's teachings. This path is often framed within a narrative of caution and encouragement, where the specter of eternal consequences serves both as a warning and a motivational tool.

However, reflecting on these structured experiences and teachings prompts a crucial inquiry: How closely do these align with Jesus' focus? Unlike the external, activity-centered approach of modern church practices, Jesus taught the importance of an inner spiritual life, which will, in time, impact our outer lives. His message emphasized a direct, personal connection with the Divine, a journey inward rather than adherence to outward religious observances and doctrines.

None of these external activities serve Jesus's one purpose: living from your inner life of spirit. Nor do these things relate to what Jesus taught or did.

At its core, religion directs our gaze outward — to prescribed behaviors, established beliefs, the edifice of organizational structures, and the daunting image of an angry God.

In contrast, spirituality invites us inward, encouraging us to explore the depths of our own spirit, where we find ourselves already in intimate union with the Divine life.

Breaking free from Churchianity is not about leaving Christ. It is about focusing on and embracing the Christ life that lives within you and abandoning the outward focus of Christianity that has manipulated and controlled people through fear and self-loathing.

GO INWARD FIRST

Everything Jesus did outwardly originated from a deep, inward wellspring of spirituality. To put it plainly, every outward expression and miracle from Christ's life was a direct result of His inward spiritual focus on the union and oneness He shared with God the Father.

> *"Life is spiritual. Your physical existence doesn't contribute to that life. The words that I have spoken to you are spiritual. They are life."* John 6:63 GW

> *"Don't you believe that I am in the Father and the Father is in me? What I'm telling you doesn't come from me. The Father, who lives in me, does what he wants."* John 14:10 GW

> *"On that day you will know that I am in my Father and that you are in me and that I am in you."* John 14:20 GW

The focal point of our existence should be Christ, not the external rituals and behaviors often emphasized by the church.

Christ's teachings emphasize a priority that has often been overshadowed: the significance of our inner spiritual life over external religious acts. The church has historically placed great importance on outward behaviors to the detriment of who we are internally as a spirit. Yet, it is crucial to remember that we are spiritual beings at our core. We possess a soul and experience life on earth in a physical body, but fundamentally, who we are is a spirit.

The shift from a traditional Christian framework to a state of spiritual liberation is essentially an inward journey, placing the spirit at the forefront of our existence. This transition represents an awakening, a soulful realization that our essence transcends this world's physical and temporal aspects.

> "While we do not look at the things which are seen, but at the things which are not seen. For the things which are seen are *temporary, but the things which* are *not seen are eternal."* II Corinthians 4:18 NKJV

Acknowledging that our true essence is spirit leads to the understanding that our outward engagements should deepen our connection with our spirit. Traditional church teachings and rituals, however, often overlook essential practices such as meditation and contemplation, mindfulness — which is living fully in the moment — and the art of "listening prayer," or listening to the Spirit.

Embarking on this inward journey is vital for spiritual health and freedom. It enables us to transcend the superficiality of religious rituals, inviting us into a realm of deep spiritual communion.

My own process of deconstructing traditional religious beliefs led me to embrace the finished work of God in Christ and every person's inclusion in that work. This reality of union brought me back to the inner reality of our spiritual unity in Christ, where we are not divided into separate entities but exist as one with Him. This is not a metaphorical unity but an indisputable, intrinsic oneness.

> "But he who is joined to the Lord is one spirit with Him." I Corinthians 6:17 NKJV

In this unity with Christ, there is no division, no separation between us and the Divine, only an all-encompassing oneness. Not two spirits, but one with the Lord — complete and absolute.

This mystical union of all things in Christ has freed me to love each person, regardless of differences in appearance, belief, or background. We are one in the Divine Life. It is within this shared life in the Divine that we find our truest connection with each other — one of love, surpassing all barriers and divisions.

LEARN TO LOVE YOURSELF

Loving another person starts with loving yourself. It is impossible to love another person until you first love the person God made you to be. In my previous book, *Alignment of Authentic Love: Living Your Highest Life*, I wrote about the importance of first loving yourself.

> *Before we become aware of who others are and see them with understanding and compassion, we must first become aware of ourselves, understanding who we are in Christ with love and compassion for ourselves. The life of Christ that is one with your spirit is agape love. Therefore, you are also agape love. You do not have to work it up or try to exert yourself, which is where we stumble the most. Everything we need is within us in Christ, including the ability to love. However, we focus externally, not internally in spirit. This means we look outside ourselves based on how we feel about ourselves rather than the inner person in Christ. This results in judgments about self, others, and God rather than enjoying God's unconditional love and loving ourselves and others.*

The direction of your focus is a predictor of what will eventually manifest in your life. Focusing on what you think is wrong with you will cause that very thing to manifest even more. If you live with the lie "there is something wrong with me," you will see something wrong not only in yourself but in every person you encounter, thus making it difficult to love anyone. You will see people in the worst possible light because you see yourself in the worst possible light. Judgment and condemnation of yourself becomes judgment and condemnation of others.

Loving yourself — embracing your spirit, soul, and body — is crucial for overcoming the self-loathing that was instilled by certain church teachings. Without this foundation of love for oneself, every relationship, including the one with yourself, risks being warped by negative perceptions.

Stepping away from the doctrine of original sin and the fear of an angry God marked the beginning of deep internal healing for me. I moved from a state of self-loathing, rooted in the belief that "there is something inherently wrong with me," to embracing self-love, recognizing the real me as created in the very image and likeness of God and as something "very good" (Genesis 1:26). This shift allowed me to see myself through a lens of Divine Love rather than judgment, gradually dissolving my fears of a constantly wrathful and disappointed God. I realized that my perceived failures to adhere to "the rules" did not diminish God's love for me.

Some rules or guidelines exist that inherently express love toward others, and these deserve our respect and adherence. However, not all imposed restrictions align with this principle of love. The heart of God is not fixated on our compliance with rules, standards, or laws; instead, His primary concern is the cultivation and expression of love.

To love others unconditionally, I first had to learn to love myself, moving beyond years of religious teachings that left me feeling unworthy and flawed. I could not shake the thought that there was something wrong with me, that Jesus needed to die in my place because of my sins. Over time, the Spirit helped me realize that I was not in Christ due to a childhood prayer I prayed to invite Jesus into my heart as a kid. I wasn't in Christ because of a decision or an act of "faith" on my part. I was in Christ, one with Him, because the Father put me there (SEE PSALMS 139:16, JOHN 14:20, EPHESIANS 1:4) apart from my efforts or theological beliefs.

Christ's faithfulness in His life, death, and resurrection confirms our union. Being one with Christ, as co-heirs with Him (ROMANS 8:17), signifies that we share in all that He is at this very moment, and likewise, He shares in all that we are (1 JOHN 4:17). This mystical union irrevocably establishes my identity, worth, and acceptance as God's child. Nothing can separate me from the love of God (ROMANS 8:38-39). If God can love me that way, in union with Him, then I am empowered to love and accept myself, to forgive myself, recognizing that I am His masterpiece (EPHESIANS 2:10). This realization enables me to love others as they are, understanding that they, too, share in this union with Him (COLOSSIANS 1:16-17).

EMBRACE THE POSSIBILITIES

In quantum physics, particles can exist in a state known as superposition. This means particles can be in multiple states simultaneously until observed or measured, defying classical intuition. In this state, particles blend all possible outcomes, offering a vast array of possibilities.

These endless possibilities already exist as mathematical probabilities within the quantum wave (unseen) function. When an observation or measurement is made, the wave function collapses, and the particles assume a specific state (seen). Until then, the particles' possible states are all equally real in quantum mechanics.

This concept hints at a universe teeming with potential, where countless scenarios and events coexist, waiting to be actualized. While these possibilities are in a state of superposition, they represent the unfathomable diversity and limitless potential that underlies the fundamental fabric of reality.

Loving yourself and others unlocks endless possibilities. When you close yourself off to those who are not like you, disagree with you, or do things you don't agree with, it closes the door to these possibilities. Because With God, all things are possible.

> "But Jesus looked at them and said, 'With men it is *impossible*, but not with God; for with God all things are possible.'"
> Mark 10:27 NKJV

In quantum physics, the observer's attention contributes to the desired outcome. What we focus on influences the result. By observing, we transform potential energy into actual matter, shaping reality. Can you see the potential and the possibilities when you turn your focus to love? Nothing is impossible with God. Love unlocks potential and liberates us from self-judgment and criticism of others. Everything is as it should be now; anything is possible if you can see it.

Letting go of a theology that requires being right all the time or separating yourself from others and embracing love opens this door.

A recent Supreme Court case involved a Christian bakery owner and a gay couple who wanted to order a cake for their wedding. The owner refused, citing her belief that it violated her religious convictions. The gay couple saw this as discrimination. Ultimately, the bakery owner won the case, believing she defended a principle aligned with her faith. Yet, is that the truth, and was she really the winner?

Under the new covenant, we are free from the old covenant law even though Gentiles were never under the Mosaic law. Nothing in the new covenant prevents a Christian or follower of Christ from baking a cake for a gay couple's wedding.

Jesus often spent much of His time with people the religious leaders labeled as sinners. He spent several days in a Samaritan town after His encounter with the woman at the well, despite Samaritans being viewed by Jews as half-breeds and heretics. Jesus mingled and interacted with people from every corner of society, driven by His mission that all people might have life and have it more abundantly (John 10:10).

Imagine the possibilities if the bakery owner approached the situation with more vision and imagination. Suppose she had agreed to bake the cake? This decision could have opened the door to getting to know the couple on a personal level, creating a space for a conversation that might increase her understanding of them and their understanding of her. Such interaction might have led to friendship, an invitation to their wedding, and the chance for her to meet others with diverse backgrounds and perspectives. Viewing the world through a lens of love, compassion, and mercy, she might have broadened her customer base and found new opportunities to share the love of Christ with a wider community. Instead, she chose a course opposite of the way of Christ and how He lived His life: one marked by fear, judgment, and exclusion of those different from her in belief and lifestyle. This approach, more aligned with rigid religious doctrine than the inclusive love of Christ, ultimately contributes to division and harm.

The love of Christ frees us to be ourselves and stop taking life so seriously. Nothing is that serious. Life presents us with opportunities to love, be loved, and grow through our mistakes and failures. We aren't under the scrutiny of an angry God who is tallying our missteps. Instead, we are given the precious opportunity to embrace those deemed unlovable and to encourage and lift up those who are disheartened. Where religion closes off possibility, spirituality embraces endless possibilities.

LIVE IN THE MOMENT

Throughout my years immersed in evangelical Christianity; I never heard a sermon on the practice of mindfulness or simply living in the moment. While teachings from Matthew 6:25-34 occasionally touched on managing anxiety and worry, especially about everyday concerns, they stopped short of advocating living in the moment. Why?

This omission of the practice of mindfulness might be rooted in the emphasis on sins, personal failings before God, and the belief that these missteps signify a deeper flaw within us. Furthermore, if you are taught to fear a God who is angry and waiting for an opportunity to punish sin, or if you are haunted by doubts about salvation — fearing loss of salvation for ongoing sins, or worse, suspecting you were never truly saved (a particularly distressing notion from my own upbringing) — then it is nearly impossible to embrace the present without fear of Divine retribution or future judgment. All of this makes living in the moment elusive.

Despite the rich tradition of monasticism, emphasizing holiness, prayer, and simplicity, the broader Christian community has not valued the practice of living in the moment. Yet, living in the moment based on how God and Christ described themselves seems to be a focus from the earliest revelation of the Divine to Israel to the time of Christ.

> *"And God said to Moses, 'I AM WHO I AM.' And He said, 'Thus you shall say to the children of Israel, I AM has sent me to you.'"* Exodus 3:14 NKJV

> *"Then Jesus spoke to them again, saying, 'I am the light of the world. He who follows Me shall not walk in darkness, but have the light of life.'"* John 8:12 NKJV

> *"Jesus said to them, 'Most assuredly, I say to you, before Abraham was, I AM.'"* John 8:58 NKJV

When Moses wanted to know God's name to convey to Israel, God responded, "I AM sent me to you." This declaration, "I AM," suggests an emphasis on the present moment. Jesus echoed this and stated, "I AM the light of the world," using "I AM" *(ego eimi* in Greek) not only to identify with the Godhead but also to express a philosophy of existence centered on the present. This implies that God lives in the now, not tethered to the past or preoccupied with the future. While God is aware of both the past and future, His focus is firmly on the present now. Jesus is the light of the world, not just historically or futuristically, but right now. Despite the emphasis on His I AM presence in scripture, most Christians do not live present in the I AM moment.

Breaking free from the grip of living in the regrets of the past or fearing the future can be challenging. Our autonomic nervous system, designed to protect us from perceived threats, can keep us in constant vigilance if we have experienced hurt or trauma. This often leads to an emotional roller coaster, with little relief from the religious dos and do nots or perceived expectations from God.

It is not uncommon for clients to come into my office and express feelings of regret for past actions and an inability to forgive themselves. They worry about how their past actions might provoke God and impact those they love. Religion feeds this by reinforcing the notion of a God angry with their failures and mistakes. Life for them is a constant roller coaster of regret, fear, and confession. They struggle to find peace in the finished work of Christ and love themselves for who they are, accepting the past as it is, learning from it, and trusting God for the future so that they may focus on the moment.

Living in the moment is where we find God, for the present is all we truly possess. Embracing the here and now is the first step toward experiencing spiritual freedom in Christ's finished work. This is the place of inner peace and rest, which is yours and every person's spiritual inheritance in Christ Jesus.

Meditation is a wonderful place to begin this journey of living in the moment. Starting with just five minutes a day to clear your mind and concentrate on breathing can open the door to enjoying the security and safety found in God's unwavering love. Breathe in, and slowly breathe out any fear, anxiety, self-loathing, and judgment you may have. With each breath, let go of fear, anxiety, and self-judgment, and embrace the peace of being loved by God unconditionally. Reflecting on scriptures that affirm His love can reinforce your worthiness in His eyes, apart from any effort or work on your part. Gradually increase these five minutes to ten minutes. In time, you'll begin to release much of the stress and anxiety religion has piled on you and relax in the arms of a good God who has always loved you just as you are.

THE POWER OF LOVE

"The Power of Love" by Huey Lewis and the News is an iconic 1985 hit that became synonymous with the classic 1980s sound. Co-written by the band and renowned songwriter Chris Hayes, it was created for the soundtrack of the blockbuster film "Back to the Future." The song perfectly captured the spirit of the movie and its themes of love, time travel, and nostalgia. The song's popularity was spectacular, reaching number one on the Billboard Hot 100 chart in the United States and earning the band their first Grammy Award nomination.

Its infectious melody, catchy lyrics, and the distinctive voice of Huey Lewis combined to create a timeless track that continues to resonate with audiences today. Lyrically, "The Power of Love" explores love's transformative and all-encompassing nature. The lyrics convey the idea that love has the power to conquer challenges and transcend time and space. The phrase — "that's the power of love" — emphasizes love's strength to overcome adversity.

If the world understands the power of love, which is the Divine Life, and every person is in union with that Life, why does Christianity not understand love's power? For millennia, the church has emphasized everything except that which Jesus emphasized in His life, death, and resurrection: love. The scriptures have made it clear that the power of love is the spirit of Christ at work to impact people. All are His children, and all are loved.

> "'I have loved you the same way the Father has loved me. So live in my love.'" John 15:9 GW

> "'I'm giving you a new commandment: Love each other in the same way that I have loved you. Everyone will know that

you are my disciples because of your love for each other.'"
John 13:34-35 GW

"'In the past God allowed all people to live as they pleased. Yet, by doing good, he has given evidence of his existence. He gives you rain from heaven and crops in their seasons. He fills you with food and your lives with happiness.'" Acts 14:16-17 GW

"Certainly, we live, move, and exist because of him. As some of your poets have said, 'We are God's children.'" Acts 17:28 GW

"Who shall separate us from the love of Christ? Shall tribulation, or distress, or persecution, or famine, or nakedness, or peril, or sword? ...Yet in all these things we are more than conquerors through Him who loved us. For I am persuaded that neither death nor life, nor angels nor principalities nor powers, nor things present nor things to come, nor height nor depth, nor any other created thing, shall be able to separate us from the love of God which is in Christ Jesus our Lord." Romans 8:35, 37-39 NKJV

"Love suffers long and is kind; love does not envy; love does not parade itself, is not puffed up; does not behave rudely, does not seek its own, is not provoked, thinks no evil; does not rejoice in iniquity, but rejoices in the truth; bears all things, believes all things, hopes all things, endures all things. Love never fails..." I Corinthians 13:4-8 NKJV

"For the love of Christ compels us, because we judge thus: that if One died for all, then all died; and He died for all, that those who live should live no longer for themselves, but for Him who died for them and rose again. Therefore, from now on, we regard no one according to the flesh. Even though

> we have known Christ according to the flesh, yet now we know Him thus no longer." II Corinthians 5:14-16 NKJV

> "I have been crucified with Christ, and it is no longer I who live, but Christ lives in me. So the life I now live in the body, I live because of the faithfulness of the Son of God, who loved me and gave himself for me." Galatians 2:20 NET

> "For you were called to freedom, brothers and sisters; only do not use your freedom as an opportunity to indulge your flesh, but through love serve one another. For the whole law can be summed up in a single commandment, namely, 'You must love your neighbor as yourself.'" Galatians 5:13-14 NET

> "But God, being rich in mercy, because of his great love with which he loved us, even though we were dead in transgressions, made us alive together with Christ — by grace you are saved! — and he raised us up with him and seated us with him in the heavenly realms in Christ Jesus, to demonstrate in the coming ages the surpassing wealth of his grace in kindness toward us in Christ Jesus." Ephesians 2:4-7 NET

> "For we are His workmanship, created in Christ Jesus for good works, which God prepared beforehand that we should walk in them." Ephesians 2:10 NKJV

We could list many other scriptures, but these are sufficient to make the point. What matters to God is love. Love is His promise over everything, including Christian doctrines, dogma, traditions, organizations, positions, statements of faith, baptism, giving, behavior, or anything else. Love changes the human heart; it is the language of every person you'll ever meet. Love is who God is.

> *"Beloved, let us love one another, for love is of God; and everyone who loves is born of God and knows God. He who does not love does not know God, for God is love."* I John 4:7-8 NKJV

There's no fear in love because perfect love, God, casts out fear (I JOHN 4:18).

I have re-examined my beliefs and allowed the Holy Spirit to reshape my theology around the central truth that God is love. I have come to understand that God loves me unconditionally, without any expectations on God's part. This realization frees me to love myself as I am and embrace all my mistakes and failures of the past. It also opens the door to loving others, recognizing that as He loves me, He also loves them, just as they are.

This was the message to my heart on this difficult journey, "I love you, Scott, more than you will ever know. I love you. Just sit, enjoy it, and soak in my love." I thought I knew He loved me, but I did not.

God's love had been shrouded by the two messages of religion: "There is something wrong with me" and "We must fear God and others." As the reality of union and oneness took hold, those chains were broken, and I was set free to be myself and love others just as they are right now. I no longer needed to "fix" myself or anyone else. I was completely free to love.

This is the gospel's message: You are loved unconditionally, just as you are, in the image and likeness of God, as demonstrated through Christ Jesus. Would you return the kiss of the one who loves you? It is really that simple. Yet, Christianity has overcomplicated this straightforward message, reshaping it to suit religious agendas and purposes through the ages.

Jesus's encounter with the woman caught in adultery illustrates the power of love. Religious leaders presented her to Jesus as a test, citing Mosaic law, which demanded her stoning. Jesus responded by writing in the sand. What was He writing? Some suggest He was listing the wrongs those leaders had done. No one knows with certainty.

Once finished, Christ stood up and said, "Whoever is without sin, let Him cast the first stone." From oldest to youngest, those leaders slowly dropped the stones they held and walked away. The oldest, possibly because they knew of their many transgressions, and finally, the youngest, possibly due to the pride of admitting guilt. Regardless of the reasons, they all left. Only Jesus and the woman remained.

Jesus asked her, "Woman, where are those who accuse you? Has no one condemned you?" "No one, Lord," the woman responded. Jesus said, "Neither do I condemn you, go and sin no more." Jesus loved people unconditionally without any hidden agendas, not aiming to change, manipulate, or control them. He loved and accepted them just as they were, without condemnation or judgment, because that is who He is. And that is who you are, even if it's hard to recognize. That life of Love lives in you, and you exist within this life of God.

The transition from religious constraints to spiritual freedom takes some time and is a process. However, love is worth it. Let the Spirit lead and guide you on this adventure of love, unveiling in you a richer, fuller experience of life than previously imagined.

13

OPEN-MINDEDNESS UNLOCKS THE DOOR TO SPIRITUAL FREEDOM

People are very open-minded about new things — as long as they're exactly like the old ones.
Charles Kettering

Evangelical churches have taught that open-mindedness can lead to trouble, not only with God but within the church community. This stems from a belief that their own theological views are correct while others are not, leading to closed-mindedness and judgment. Such a viewpoint prevents the exploration of spiritual freedom, confining beliefs within the rigid boundaries of the church's doctrines. The inclination to remain within one's religious tribe or denomination, alongside like-minded individuals, and the fear of challenging established norms are key reasons why many resist theological and spiritual change despite internal prompts to explore and question.

A willingness to explore and learn has aided me in theological deconstruction and spiritual awakening. Embracing openness has fostered humility, revealing that I do not hold all the answers. I have learned that individuals outside our religious community have valuable insights to offer. Listening without fear and trusting in the Spirit's guidance allow us to grow and learn from diverse perspectives.

QUANTUM PHYSICS AND SPIRITUALITY

Albert Einstein's equation $E=mc^2$ is a fundamental concept in his theory of special relativity. It relates energy (E) to mass (m) and the speed of light (c), where "c" represents the speed of light in a vacuum, approximately 186,282 miles per second. In simple terms, the equation tells us that energy and mass are interchangeable, revealing that mass is just a dense form of energy. Consequently, even a small amount of mass can unleash a tremendous amount of energy.[1]

Nuclear reactions like those fueling the sun or powering nuclear plants illustrate Einstein's $E=mc^2$ perfectly by converting a minuscule amount of mass into a massive amount of energy.[2] It explains how a small amount of mass can result in a substantial release of energy, as seen in the operation of atomic bombs. This equation revolutionized our understanding of the relationship between matter and energy, showing two sides of the same coin and paving the way for significant scientific and technological advancements.

How does this proven theory impact theology and spirituality? By suggesting that all of creation, as understood through science, is a manifestation of God's revelation. This understanding that everything is fundamentally energy in vibration — whether visible as matter or invisible — challenges us to reconsider the nature of reality itself. It suggests that the tangible world around us, while seemingly solid and permanent, is actually a transient state of energy.

The world of material things around us is an elaborate illusion, like a theatrical play with props and costumes, all of which are forms of energy condensed into matter. This matter, which shapes our reality, will, in time, revert to its original, unseen energy form. Our thoughts and feelings also manifest this energy — neural connections and chemical reactions in response to various stimuli, all rooted in energy.

Science illuminates this fundamental truth: The foundation of everything is unseen energy, temporarily transformed into the material world we interact with. This understanding reveals that what we perceive with our senses is a material expression of a much deeper, invisible energy field.

Ninety-five percent of all energy is invisible, leaving only five percent of the universe as the matter we can see and touch. The same is true of life in the Spirit. It is the unseen that is more significant, not the material. In the grand scheme, the material world is five percent of everything in God's economy, while the unseen spiritual realm represents the vast majority of reality. Should we concentrate on the tangible five percent, or should we direct our attention to the unseen ninety-five percent, which, although invisible, forms the essence of existence? This question challenges us to consider the value we place on the material versus the spiritual, prompting a deeper exploration of where the true significance lies.

EXPANDING REVELATION ABOUT OUR UNIVERSE

The James Webb Telescope launched on December 25, 2021, and now orbits over a million miles from Earth. It has been a window to the cosmos, unveiling breathtaking images of distant stars, galaxies, and nebulae unseen before. In one of its first photos, the telescope captured an image of an area of space as minuscule as the size of a grain of sand held at arm's length, revealing numerous previously invisible galaxies obscured by the glare of the brighter ones.[3] This glimpse into the vastness of the universe places our Earth and the solar system in a humbling perspective, emphasizing our material insignificance in the cosmic expanse.

How might this impact our theology and spirituality? These discoveries have reinforced the reality that Earth is a small part of an infinite universe. While God cares deeply about me, my struggles are relatively insignificant to creation and God's power. Keeping things in perspective is productive. It also helps to see that the God who made this immense, amazing, beautiful universe is more concerned with love, mercy, compassion, and understanding than with judgment and punishment.

THE SCAPEGOAT MECHANISM AND THE MURDER OF CHRIST

René Girard (1923-2015), a French-American historian, literary critic, and philosopher, introduced the influential concept of mimetic theory. Girard's mimetic theory posits that human desire and behavior are deeply influenced by imitation. He suggests that individuals tend to want what others want, leading to competition and conflict over limited resources or goals. This imitation of desires can result in a cycle of escalating rivalry and violence.[4]

The scapegoat mechanism is a central concept in Girard's theory. It describes a way for societies to temporarily alleviate internal conflicts by redirecting collective aggression onto a chosen scapegoat. When tensions and violence reach a breaking point, a community identifies a scapegoat, often an individual or a group, as the source of its troubles. This sacrificial victim is blamed for the problems, and the community unites against them, releasing built-up tension and re-establishing social cohesion.

The scapegoat mechanism can be found in various aspects of human history and culture, from religious rituals to political scapegoating. Girard believed that understanding this mechanism is essential for recognizing and eventually transcending the destructive cycles of mimetic desire and violence in human societies.

He saw the crucifixion of Jesus as a picture of this cycle. The Jewish religious leaders felt threatened by Jesus' growing popularity and the miracles He performed, fearing they would lose their influence over the people and their standing with the Roman authorities. In other words, they wanted what Jesus had: the attention and adoration of the people. This drove them to envy and fear, culminating in their decision to blame Him for societal tendencies, leading to His crucifixion.

In choosing Jesus as a scapegoat, they followed a pattern seen in the ancient Jewish tradition of releasing a scapegoat on the Day of Atonement, symbolizing the removal of the community's sins. By attributing their problems to Jesus and orchestrating His crucifixion, Jewish leaders sought to eliminate the source of their envy and restore their own positions of power and control. This act of making Jesus the scapegoat was not only to rid themselves of a rival but also to recapture the people's attention and devotion by blaming Him for their problems, murdering Him, and taking what was rightfully His.

This scapegoat mechanism can be seen in every people group, tribe, religion, and political system. It helps explain not only the murder of Christ by the Jews but also the understanding that our desires are impacted by what we believe other people value.

For instance, if someone at work has a chair and appears to value it, we believe it has value, so we also want it. But there is only one chair. The ensuing tensions and conflict result in a need for a scapegoat. The individuals involved may find a third party to blame for not ordering more chairs and seek to have them fired or punished. Either way, the scapegoating ends the conflict, and order is restored.

This gives us a greater understanding of humanity, the Bible, Christ's murder, and daily life with people in neighborhoods, cities, and nations.

We value something because others see it as valuable. Our desires are influenced from outside us rather than within us in spirit. The soul then desires, covets, and ultimately is willing to commit murder, eventually expressing itself in an action toward another person.

NEAR-DEATH EXPERIENCES AND THE REALITY OF GOD'S LOVE

Near-death experiences (NDEs) are profoundly transformative encounters that some individuals report after briefly dying and then being resuscitated. While the exact number of recorded NDEs is challenging to quantify, they have been documented worldwide, with millions of accounts.[5]

Typical NDEs often involve a sequence of common elements: a sense of leaving the physical body, moving through a tunnel or into a bright light, encountering deceased loved ones or a transcendent being, feeling an overwhelming sense of peace and love, and sometimes a life review. Many individuals describe a newfound perspective on life and a reduced fear of death after such an experience. For those who have undergone them, NDEs often lead to a shift in personal values, with an increased focus on love, compassion, and interconnectedness.[6]

Near-death experiences (NDEs) can challenge certain aspects of Christian theology, particularly concerning the afterlife, judgment, and the nature of God's mercy. Some Christian traditions teach that salvation is conditional upon repentance and faith in Jesus Christ. However, NDEs tend to contradict this, as every person seems to experience acceptance, love, inclusion, and mercy, irrespective of their religious beliefs or life actions. This universal experience of the goodness of God during NDEs calls into question the exclusivity associated with Christian doctrines of salvation. Most NDE accounts include encounters with a loving and non-judgmental Light or Presence, which seems at odds with conventional Christian beliefs about a final judgment. A small minority have darker experiences, but even then, when they cry out to God, they are delivered.

NDEs sometimes involve encounters with deceased loved ones, which could be seen as a form of communication with the dead, potentially challenging Christian views on the nature of the afterlife and the possibility of such interactions.

While NDEs do not necessarily negate Christian theology, they do introduce interesting theological questions, especially regarding the inclusivity of Divine grace and the nature of God's judgment and mercy. As a result, these experiences have prompted some Christians to reconsider and adapt their beliefs to accommodate the accounts of people experiencing NDEs.

These experiences are also part of God's general revelation and should be considered to understand specific revelation fully. Modern technology, especially regarding heart attack victims, has allowed medicine to bring people back from the dead — some even after ten to fifteen minutes. What they experience has changed many of their lives, similar to a conversion. Their attempt to express an all-encompassing love, compassion, and acceptance beyond understanding is moving and exhilarating. It is impossible to listen to these and not grasp the credibility and legitimacy behind them.

Each account is a little different, yet each has a common theme of unconditional love and peace. These testimonies of God's unconditional love for all people have impacted how I view God, myself, and others. They have helped me reflect and adjust my theology about judgment, punishment, and condemnation from an "angry God."

UNLOCKING THE DOOR

The key to growth is openness to ideas that challenge your current beliefs about scripture and life. True maturity involves being open-minded, willing to change, and ready to explore new perspectives that test your convictions. This process leads to a deeper understanding of your completeness in the Divine, fostering humility, patience towards differing views, and a profound inner peace. Embarking on this journey promises spiritual freedom like never before.

These things have assisted me in my spiritual journey of deconstructing my beliefs and reconstructing them with greater insight and understanding. Many other areas have been of help, such as the study of Christianity's place in history, warts and all. It is helpful to read from historians who are not evangelical Christians and their insights into Christian history and its place in the development of Western culture.

Are you open to something that may not agree with your understanding and interpretation of scripture and life in general? This is the mark of maturity. Maturity is not being closed-minded and demanding that everyone believe as you do. It is by changing and growing and being open to new things that not only challenge your beliefs but force you to test them rigorously. I hope that you will begin this incredible journey and experience for yourself this spiritual freedom that is your inheritance in Christ.

AFTERWORD

The dogmas of the quiet past are inadequate to the stormy present. The occasion is piled high with difficulty, and we must rise with the occasion. As our case is new, so we must think anew and act anew.

Abraham Lincoln

America's shifting demographics are poised to significantly alter institutional Christianity in the next twenty-five years. The Baby Boomer generation (born between 1946 and 1964), which currently constitutes the largest church-going demographic, is entering retirement years, with the oldest members beginning to pass away. Gen X (born between 1965 and 1980), following the Boomers, represents a smaller percentage of church attendees.

A more pronounced shift is seen with the Millennials (those born from 1981 to 1997) and Gen Z (those born from 1998 to 2012), many of whom are distancing themselves from organized religion, opting instead for alternative ways to express their spirituality. This trend is expected to continue, especially with advancements in technology and a more fragmented culture.[1]

The group of "nones" (those without a religious affiliation) and "dones" (those who have left Christianity) already accounts for over twenty-seven percent of all American adults and is growing. The figure is expected to rise to thirty-seven percent by 2030. Such changes forecast a decline in church attendance and a reduction in the number of congregations, marking a transformative period for Christianity in America.[2]

Will organized institutional Christian religion continue to exist in America? Yes. It will continue, albeit smaller, and look very different in the decades to come as it tries to meet societal changes it has resisted or ignored for far too long. Hopefully, by then, it will become more tolerant, less dogmatic, less political, and more loving. By 2050, Christians are expected to comprise less than fifty percent of the population, positioning those who identify as Christians as a minority.

The shift away from traditional organized religion is likely to be by individuals who prioritize their spiritual life over external religious practices. People finding spiritual freedom through a direct connection with the life of God within themselves will not rely on external religious structures like pastors, buildings, or denominations to guide beliefs and actions.

This movement toward spirituality allows for freedom to be yourself and to express your unique person. This freedom enhances external relationships by reducing judgment, criticism, rejection, and intolerance. I pray I live to see this transition in our society and that this book will help in that transition!

My spiritual journey, including theological deconstruction and reconstruction, continues. Choosing to step away from institutional Christianity while maintaining a connection to Christ is a path I have taken, but it is not prescriptive for everyone. Such decisions are deeply personal and are between you and the Spirit of all life.

Living in a community with other spiritually minded people is important, especially as more people re-evaluate their theological beliefs and grow spiritually. Technology has played a key role in creating new forms of connections that look different from the traditional concept of "church." It is an exciting time to be alive and to witness this transition.

THINGS THAT KEEP YOU STUCK

As you navigate from religious bondage toward spiritual freedom, it is important to recognize potential obstacles that might hinder your progress. Understanding these challenges can provide clarity and direction, helping you overcome them in your personal spiritual journey.

Religious Codependency

As a response to the Christian doctrine of original sin, which posits that God is displeased with everyone due to an inherent flaw in human nature, I have observed a trend of religious codependency among Christians. This observation stems from my experiences as a pastor and spiritual counselor. Religious codependency, in this context, refers to a reliance on external religious structures or figures for validation, forgiveness, and a sense of worth, driven by the belief in a fundamental separation from God due to sin.

Below is a diagram I use with clients to explain the dynamics of religious codependency and how it impacts them.

Figure 12.1

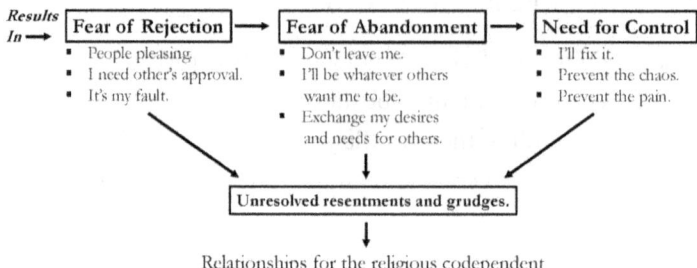

Relationships for the religious codependent
are primarily based on **fear** rather than **love**.

Individuals experiencing religious codependency struggle with a deep-seated fear rooted in the belief of an angry God, potential disapproval from their religious community, and the anxiety of being misled or deceived. All of this is hard-wired (or deeply ingrained) into their emotional fabric the longer they remain with the religious group, leading to pervasive feelings of self-loathing. Self-loathing stems from a shame-based self-concept, a consequence of being taught that there is something inherently wrong with them. Shame whispers the lie that one is deeply flawed at their core instead of understanding that making mistakes is normal and does not mean they are not a good person. Fear is the driving emotion in every relationship and action, creating a cycle of dependency and diminished self-worth.

If you choose to remain in your church, please realize that it may continue to feed this cycle.

- Fear of rejection can turn to people-pleasing and seeking the approval of others, especially those in leadership.
- Fear of abandonment can result in not being yourself or putting on a "mask" at church for fear people will not approve of you and will ultimately leave you.
- To avoid pain, the religious codependent tries to fix what is perceived to be wrong with themselves by working through discipleship programs, trying harder to have a good marriage, volunteering relentlessly, "being" there for others, or acting as a loyal soldier for the organization. All of this replaces who the person actually is to avoid the pain and chaos that could occur if they were just themselves.

Sadly, many relationships in religious settings are more about fear than genuine love, although exceptions exist. This fear — of rejection, being alone, and the trouble that might come from just being you — controls many people's lives without them even realizing it.

Walking away from organized religion, as the apostle Paul left Judaism, might be a crucial first step to healing. The decision does not have to be permanent and will depend on your circumstances. Recognizing the problem and the cycle it perpetuates is an excellent first step to healing and restoration.[3]

Unchallenged Beliefs

A point arrives when you must critically examine the teachings and beliefs ingrained in you by your church. Left unchallenged, these beliefs can dominate your life, preventing you from achieving the spiritual freedom necessary to be the person you were created to be in spirit and soul. In chapters seven and eight, I explored beliefs that keep us bound to religion rather than to experience the love and grace found in Christ's finished work, which already resides within us. I highlighted the issue of being more devoted to organizations and their doctrines than experiencing the transformative power of Christ's presence in our lives.

I encourage you to reread chapters seven and eight before finishing the book. Fear can be a significant barrier when challenging theological and religious beliefs we have held for many years. But theological beliefs that can't be challenged, questioned, examined, and tested are not sound; they are dogma others have taught. Clinging to these provides a false sense of security, dictating a life of following rules or standards.

I had to give myself permission to question my religious beliefs and trust that God's love for me would not waver during this period of doubt and examination. This journey led me to a deeper understanding that God is Love, and His love remains constant despite any disagreements or tensions it might cause with others.

Fear of the Unknown

Facing the uncertainty of challenging your current theological beliefs, religious traditions, and denominational structures might be the hardest part of seeking spiritual freedom. Most people dislike not knowing what will happen in any situation. Businesses, for instance, make yearly budgets to estimate their future sales, the costs involved in making those sales, and the projected profits. This planning helps them to assess the risks associated with future investments and spending. Similarly, governments evaluate risks using current data, and churches prepare budgets to estimate donations, expenses, and major spending. Both aim to assess and manage potential risks.

Questions that may arise about the repercussions of questioning deeply held beliefs:

- What will the outcome be for us and our family members if we challenge theological beliefs, religious traditions, and denominational hierarchies?
- Will we be labeled heretics and cast out of the church?
- Will we lose our friendships in the church we have spent years cultivating and enjoying?
- Where would we go to enjoy fellowship and community?

- What would the impact be on our children and extended family?

These concerns are valid and worth considering before embarking on significant shifts in belief or discussing these changes with others. The consequences of such a journey are inevitable.

Yet, reflecting on your current state of happiness and fulfillment is crucial. Are you content to remain in a place that does not align with your convictions, maintaining the status quo simply to avoid conflict and please others? Pleasing people should not be the primary reason for stifling your spiritual growth and freedom. Only you can answer this question. Remember, you cannot control others or the future; that is in God's hands. However, you can make choices based on your true values and desires, not out of fear.

I chose the road less traveled, although reluctantly at first. Some people have stopped being my friend; family members have chastised or cut me off, and even strangers have lashed out at me on social media. Yet, I have never been happier, more at rest and at peace internally, assured that I am living my purpose for being on this earth. I would not change a thing. I do not know what the future holds, but I am enjoying the moment, which is much more than I can say for my previous life in evangelical institutional Christianity.

LOVE AND TRUST

Embracing the divine life and finding joy in yourself and others hinges on unconditional love, cultivating trust in that very Life. Experiencing and knowing you are loved unconditionally — without any conditions or expectations — is crucial for building trust. The more you understand that you are loved just as you are, not for any religious actions or decisions, the easier it becomes to transition from strict religious practices to true spiritual freedom. While this concept is simple, the process can be challenging due to past experiences with religious trauma, strict doctrines, and traditions.

When I went through the initial stages of my nerve disease, it prompted a deep re-evaluation of my beliefs about God, the Bible, Christianity, and my identity. This took some time. During the first several years, everything the Spirit communicated to me was about unconditional love: from the people who helped me, the provision of finances, my wife's and my family's support to helpful YouTube videos and social media content. Everywhere I looked, I found messages of love. I needed to be loved by a good and loving God, to understand that I am accepted, valued, and loved for who I am, without any conditions and expectations from God. Even today, my spiritual focus is on how deeply the Divine loves me. This assurance is vital to me, especially after years of religious teaching that suggested I was inherently flawed and living under the fear of an angry God due to my constant failure to measure up.

Healing and restoration come solely through agape love, a love that leads you to inner rest and peace. Nothing else can nurture a willingness to trust the Spirit. This is how we were intended to live — led by the Spirit in every moment, not confined by religious texts, practices, or dogmas. Simply living a life of love. With trust in this love, incredible experiences unfold.

ENJOY YOUR JOURNEY

Finally, I encourage you to embrace and enjoy the journey life offers you. Appreciate every moment with gratitude and a thankful heart, recognizing that every moment is a precious gift. Life here on Earth is fleeting, and it is over sooner than you realize. While my journey has been unexpected at times, full of twists and turns, the people I have met and built relationships with have been the richest part of it.

Exiting Christianity, especially the evangelical traditions, could easily lead to feelings of bitterness, unforgiveness, and resentment. Yet, my interactions with evangelical Christians have helped shape me into who I am today. Life's tapestry is not merely black and white but a vibrant mix of beautiful colors, including challenging experiences. I love my evangelical Christian brethren, regardless of their feelings toward me or their views of my departure from their tribe. And it is in that love that Christ's life expresses itself. Let this deep, abiding, Agape Love who lives within you guide your journey, turning it into something greater than you can imagine.

My prayer and hope for you is that you discover, in the end, that love is all there is and all that matters.

NOTES

INTRODUCTION

1. "Modeling the Future of Religion in America: If recent trends in religious switching continue, Christians could make up less than half of the U.S. population within a few decades," Pew Research Center, last modified September 7, 2022, https://www.pewresearch.org/religion/wp-content/uploads/sites/7/2022/09/US-Religious-Projections_FOR-PRODUCTION-9.13.22.pdf., Pg. 6.
2. Phyllis Tickle, *The Great Emergence: How Christianity Is Changing And Why* (Grand Rapids: Baker Books, 2012), chap. 3, Kindle.

1. THE PARADOX OF CHRISTIAN RELIGION: "CHURCHIANITY"

1. Merriam-Webster Dictionary, https://www.merriam-webster.com/dictionary/religion. Retrieved December 11, 2022.
2. Oxford English Dictionary, https://www.oed.com/viewdictionaryentry/Entry/161944#:~:text=Categories%20%C2%BB-,a.,of%20religious%20rites%20or%20observances. Retrieved December 11, 2022.

2. RELIGIOUS CODEPENDENCY

1. Glennon Doyle. *Untamed* (New York: Random House, 2020), Pg. 15.
2. https://www.newyorker.com/magazine/2012/11/26/the-hell-raiser-3
3. Merriam-Webster Dictionary, https://www.merriam-webster.com/dictionary/codependency, retrieved February 23, 2023.
4. After researching the origins of the doctrine of Hell, the word's etymology, the underlying Greek words that are translated as Hell, and Western Christianity's use of the word, as well as in popular culture, I concluded that there is no such physical place, except in our minds, thoughts, and emotions. Hell is actually not in the Bible, as there are no Hebrew or Greek words for Hell. In an attempt to simplify understanding and support a doctrinal position, the translators translated the Hebrew word *Sheol* and the Greek words *Gehenna*, *Hades*, and *Tartarus* as Hell. *Sheol* is the word for a grave where dead bodies are buried. *Gehenna* was a trash dump outside Jerusalem. *Hades* is the place that all dead souls go to in Greek mythology, and *Tartarus* was a mythical Greek god who punished the enemy soldiers of Greece after their death. It was used once in II Peter, referring to the myth of fallen angels and what God did to them. That is it. When the word Hell is used in the New Testament

scriptures, it is usually in a parable or as a metaphor. In addition, the apostle Paul never wrote about Hell, not even a paragraph. Nor did he use the words Gehenna, Hades, or Tartarus. For a deeper dive, I encourage you to read Rob Bell's book, *Love Wins*, and Don Keithley's book, *Hell's Illusion*.

4. THE CALL TO SPIRITUAL FREEDOM

1. Peter Lord, *Turkeys and Eagles* (Jacksonville: The Seed Sowers, 1987). The book is written as a short parable and can be read in a few hours.

5. BEYOND DENOMINATIONS AND DOGMA

1. See the following video clip as an example of God's justice in action. https://www.youtube.com/watch?v=qeESVLQK4hw.
2. Scott Mautz, "Science Says This Is Why You Fear Change (and What to Do About It)." Inc., November 16, 2017, https://www.inc.com/scott-mautz/science-says-this-is-why-you-fear-change-and-what-to-do-about-it.html.
3. I am not suggesting that you have to leave your church due to this inner change of heart. Some stay with their church and continue to fellowship, even though they hold theological beliefs that continue to evolve. Some find leaving necessary to detox and deconstruct, as the apostle Paul did after his Damascus road experience. It was likely two or three years before Paul returned to Damascus from Arabia. He needed time away from everyone as he deconstructed Judaism and began to embrace the reality of his life in Christ. I found leaving was necessary for me. I have made much more progress outside the institutional church than in it. Each person is different. Let the Spirit of Christ lead you, and trust His direction.

6. LOVE HERETIC

1. Kurt Rudolph, *Gnosis: The Nature and History of Gnosticism* (San Francisco: Harper San Francisco, 1987), Pgs. 53-57.

7. RECONSIDERING CORE THEOLOGICAL BELIEFS: PART ONE

1. See Don Keithley's book, *Hell's Illusion: Exposing the Myth of Hell*, for a deeper dive into this topic. Also, see Wikipedia.com for a discussion of the etymology of the word "hell."

8. RECONSIDERING CORE THEOLOGICAL BELIEFS: PART TWO

1. Teresa Nowakowski, Webb Telescope Finds Evidence of Massive Galaxies That Defy Theories of the Early Universe, *Smithsonian Magazine*, last modified February 24, 2023, https://www.smithsonianmag.com/smart-news/webb-telescope-finds-evidence-of-massive-galaxies-that-defy-theories-of-the-early-universe-180981689/#:~:text=SMART%20NEWS,Webb%20Telescope%20Finds%20Evidence%20of%20Massive%20Galaxies,Theories%20of%20the%20Early%20Universe&text=Astronomers%20have%20identified%20what%20appear,of%20the%20origins%20of%20galaxies.
2. D. Scott Cook, *Alignment of Authentic Love: Living Your Highest Life* (Plano: Abide Publishing, 2023), Pgs. 46-47.
3. Jules Brody, "Fate, Philology, Freud." *Philosophy and Literature*, No. 38.1 (April 2014): 23.
4. D. Scott Cook, *Alignment of Authentic Love: Living Your Highest Life* (Plano: Abide Publishing, 2023), Pg. 98.

9. LEAVING THE TRIBE OF MY FATHER AND MOTHER

1. "Brainwave Entrainment," *Wikipedia*, https://en.wikipedia.org/wiki/Brainwave_entrainment. Retrieved August 21, 2023.
2. YouTube, *Synchronization of Metronomes*, https://www.youtube.com/watch?v=Aaxw4zbULMs. Retrieved 08/21/2023.

10. FREEDOM TO LOVE YOURSELF

1. Marlene Winell. *Leaving the Fold: A Guide for Former Fundamentalists and Others Leaving Their Religion*
    (Berkeley: Apocryphile Press, 2007), Pg. 1.
2. "Early Church Meriting Legalism," *Internet Bible College*, http://internetbiblecollege.net/Lessons/Early%20Church%20Meriting%20Legalism.htm#_ftn2. Retrieved September 14, 2023.
3. As discussed in chapter seven, the word for sin in Greek is hamartia, a compound word from *ha*, which means "not," and *martia*, which is from the root word mores, meaning "portion, lot, or form." So, "not your portion, lot, or form." It was originally used in ancient Greek tragedies to describe the fatal error of the protagonist due to a lack of information. It was later used to describe an archer missing the target he was shooting for because he was without vital information, such as elevation, wind direction, speed, distance to the target, or speed at which the target was moving. Missing the mark would have been an ancient understanding of hamartia. The Jews would have understood hamartia as missing the mark (as a Jew who was under the law, and then later judging Gentiles and their behavior, even though they were not under the law) of the requirements of the Mosaic law. The word "sin" is

from the old French and was used by translators to mean all the bad things someone does in their life ("be sure your sins will find you out."), yet nothing could be further from the truth regarding the meaning of this word. A better understanding would be confusion or misunderstanding. Christ came to save us from the confusion of our minds regarding our identity, God's identity, and the value of each individual (the story of Adam and Eve and the fall in Chapter Three of Genesis is a picture of this). "Greater love has no one than this than to lay down one's life for his friends." There is no better way to solve this confusion than for Jesus to submit Himself to those who are in that confusion so that they may see what love really is and, in time, that their identity was actually in the one they murdered.

13. OPEN-MINDEDNESS UNLOCKS THE DOOR TO SPIRITUAL FREEDOM

1. Bruce Rosenblum and Fred Kuttner, *Quantum Enigma: Physics Encounters Consciousness* (Oxford: Oxford University Press, 2011), Pg. 50.
2. Bruce Rosenblum and Fred Kuttner, *Quantum Enigma: Physics Encounters Consciousness* (Oxford: Oxford University Press, 2011), Pg. 50.
3. "NASA's Webb Delivers Deepest Infrared Image of Universe Yet," NASA, accessed October 19, 2023, https://www.nasa.gov/image-article/nasas-webb-delivers-deepest-infrared-image-of-universe-yet/.
4. James Williams, *The Girard Reader* (New York: Crossroad Publishing Co., 1996), Pgs. 9-10.
5. Pim van Lommel, *Consciousness Beyond Life: The Science of the Near-Death Experiences* (San Francisco: HarperOne Publishing, 2011), Chapter Two, Kindle.
6. Raymond Moody, *Life After Life* (San Francisco: HarperOne Publishing, 2015), Chapter Two, Kindle.

AFTERWORD

1. Nicholas Kristof, "America is Losing Religious Faith," New York Times, August 23, 2023, https://www.nytimes.com/2023/08/23/opinion/christianity-america-religion-secular.html.
2. "Modeling the Future of Religion in America: If recent trends in religious switching continue, Christians could make up less than half of the U.S. population within a few decades," Pew Research Center, accessed October 19, 2023, https://www.pewresearch.org/religion/wp-content/uploads/sites/7/2022/09/US-Religious-Projections_FOR-PRODUCTION-9.13.22.pdf., Pg. 7.
3. For more on this topic, please read *Codependent No More* by Melody Beattie. Because codependency is an addiction, there are Codependents Anonymous groups, or CODA, throughout the U.S. and the world that are available to those seeking recovery. Reading her book and attending a CODA group near you is a good first step out of religious codependency. Go to our website at http://www.aiagape.com to discover other services for those recovering from religious co-dependency.

ACKNOWLEDGMENTS

I am grateful for the many pastors, teachers, church members, and friends from the churches I was a part of and served vocationally. Who, over the years, were involved in the Churchianity trap as well. Without them, I would not be writing this book.

I am thankful to Southern Baptists for the years I grew in my spiritual awakening under their care. In time, I had to leave, but I would not be where I am without them.

I'm grateful to my brother Darrell, who was one of the first people to challenge my understanding of the church and the bible.

Thanks to Steve McVey and the Grace Walk Experience class that I was a part of for five years. It was a liberating experience and helped me to walk away from Churchianity.

Thanks to Robin Smit of The Writers Society, who was the managing editor and gave creative feedback on the book. But especially for her ability to make me sound like an articulate writer.

To my wife Cyndi, who reviewed each chapter for consistency and gave me creative feedback.

Finally, thanks to the many clients I have counseled over the years who have allowed me to be a part of their brave journeys out of Churchianity and into spiritual freedom.

ABOUT THE AUTHOR

Scott Cook is the Founder and President of Abiding in Agape, a spiritual counseling service, and teaching ministry dedicated to helping people come out of the fear and control of legalistic Christian religion, struggling with the trauma of the past, so they can enjoy inner rest and peace. He hosts the weekly national TV program Breaking Free From Churchianity and is the author of *Alignment of Authentic Love: Living Your Highest Life.*

Scott has over thirty years of experience in pastoral ministry, spiritual counseling, and business/professional training and coaching. He graduated from Oklahoma State University with a degree in Business and from Southwestern Baptist Theological Seminary with a Master of Divinity. Scott has taught in leadership seminars, professional training classes, churches, retreats, and conferences in the United States and other parts of the world.

Scott and his wife Cyndi, live in the Dallas area of Texas. He is the father of two adult boys and is also a grandfather.

ALSO BY SCOTT COOK

Learn to enjoy a dynamic relationship with God, come to terms with past trauma to embrace and love yourself and be free emotionally to have healthy, loving relationships with others.

Available on Amazon in hardback, paperback and kindle.

www.ingramcontent.com/pod-product-compliance
Lightning Source LLC
Chambersburg PA
CBHW070447050426
42451CB00015B/3381